# Content

# Number Word Search

**a.** Circle the correct words in the word search.

```
o  a  s  e  v  e  n  t  e  e  n  n
n  e  i  g  h  t  e  e  n  b  c  i
e  e  n  i  n  e  t  e  e  n  v  n
s  i  a  e  l  e  v  e  n  z  a  e
e  g  z  t  w  e  l  v  e  z  f  m
v  h  g  o  t  o  t  h  e  z  o  o
e  t  q  f  i  f  t  e  e  n  q  i
n  q  q  t  w  e  n  t  y  a  b  a
a  f  o  u  r  t  e  e  n  t  w  o
s  i  x  t  e  e  n  t  h  r  e  e
s  i  x  t  h  i  r  t  e  e  n  w
f  o  u  r  a  f  i  v  e  t  e  n
```

| one   | six   | eleven   | sixteen   |
|-------|-------|----------|-----------|
| two   | seven | twelve   | seventeen |
| three | eight | thirteen | eighteen  |
| four  | nine  | fourteen | nineteen  |
| five  | ten   | fifteen  | twenty    |

Chalkboard Publishing Inc © 2007

Canadian Math Basics Series  Grade 2

# Counting by 25's - 1000

**a.** Connect the dots counting by 25's to 1000.

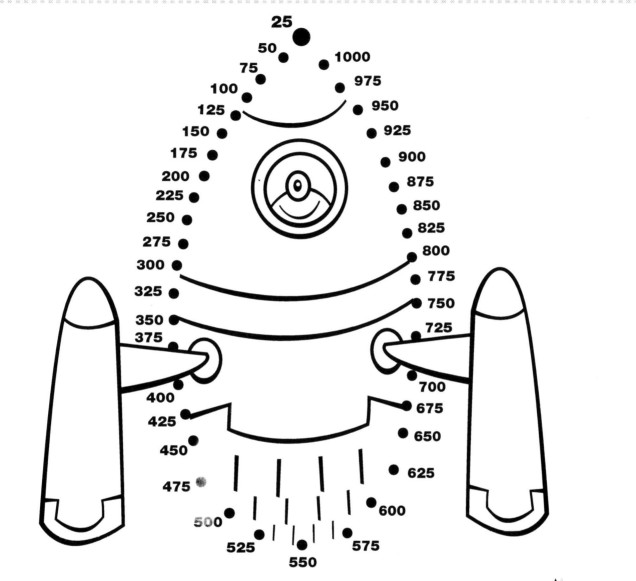

25
50
75
100
125
150
175
200
225
250
275
300
325
350
375
400
425
450
475
500
525
550
575
600
625
650
675
700
725
750
775
800
825
850
875
900
925
950
975
1000

**b. Brain Stretch:**

Count by 10's.

60, ( _____ ), ( _____ ), ( _____ ), ( _____ ), ( _____ ), ( _____ ), ( _____ ), ( _____ )

Count by 5's.

15, ( _____ ), ( _____ ), ( _____ ), ( _____ ), ( _____ ), ( _____ ), ( _____ ), ( _____ )

Count by 2's.

150, ( _____ ), ( _____ ), ( _____ ), ( _____ ), ( _____ ), ( _____ ), ( _____ ), ( _____ )

Canadian Math Basics Series  Grade 2

# Counting Backwards By 1's

**a.** Connect the dots counting backwards by 1's to 50.

**b. Brain Stretch:** Look at the number line and answer the following questions.

Number Line:
45 46 47 48 49 50 51 52 53 54 55 56 57 58 59 60 61 62 63 64 65 66 67 68 69 70

1. What numbers are between **56** and **63**?

2. What numbers are between **66** and **70**?

Chalkboard Publishing Inc © 2007

Canadian Math Basics Series  Grade 2

# Odd And Even Numbers

a. Colour the spaces with even numbers in **orange** and colour the spaces with odd numbers in **green**.

> **Math Talk: Odd and Even Numbers**
>
> Look only at the ones column to see if a number is odd or even.
>
> Odd numbers end in 1, 3 , 5 , 7, or 9
>
> Even numbers end in 0, 2 , 4 , 6, or 8

Canadian Math Basics Series  Grade 2

# Ordering Numbers

**a. Fill in the missing numbers.**

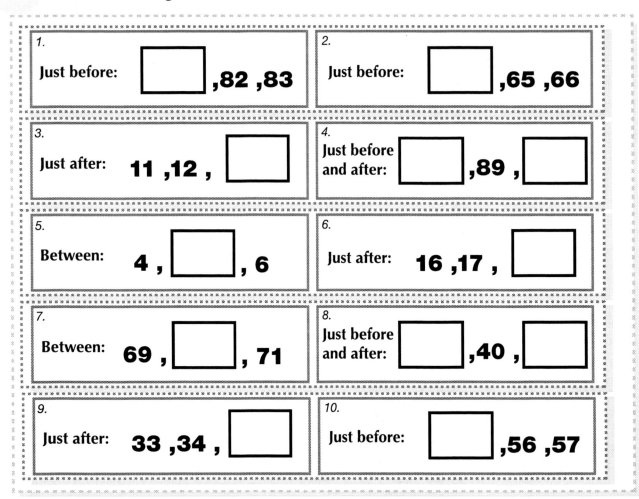

1. Just before: [ ] ,82 ,83

2. Just before: [ ] ,65 ,66

3. Just after: 11 ,12 , [ ]

4. Just before and after: [ ] ,89 , [ ]

5. Between: 4 , [ ] , 6

6. Just after: 16 ,17 , [ ]

7. Between: 69 , [ ] , 71

8. Just before and after: [ ] ,40 , [ ]

9. Just after: 33 ,34 , [ ]

10. Just before: [ ] ,56 ,57

**b. Order each group of numbers from smallest to largest.**

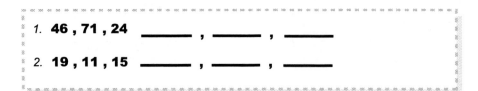

1. 54 , 29 , 71 , 18 _____ , _____ , _____ , _____

2. 39 , 63 , 3 , 84 _____ , _____ , _____ , _____

3. 6 , 69 , 92 , 46 _____ , _____ , _____ , _____

**c. Order each group of numbers from largest to smallest .**

1. 46 , 71 , 24 _____ , _____ , _____

2. 19 , 11 , 15 _____ , _____ , _____

Canadian Math Basics Series  Grade 2

# Tens And Ones

a. Count the tens and ones. Write how many blocks in all.

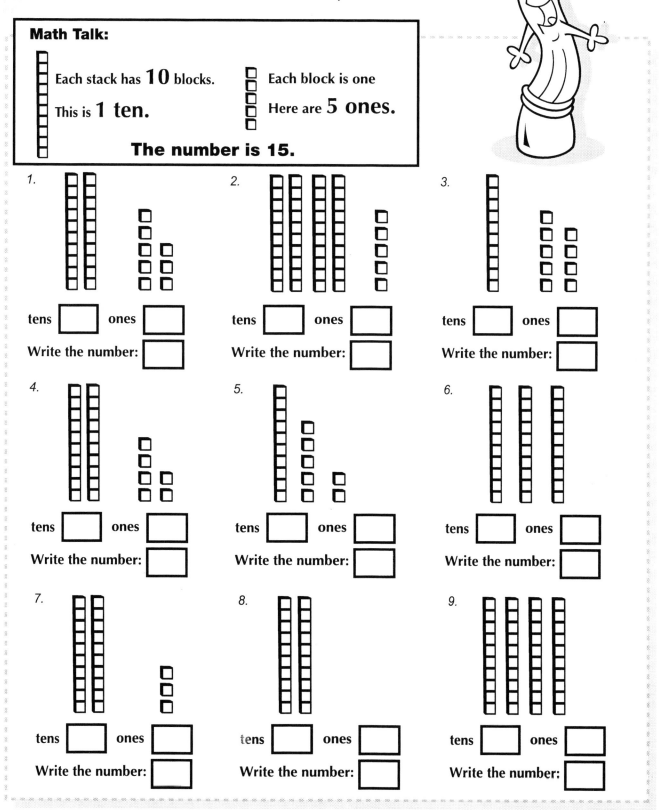

**Math Talk:**

Each stack has **10** blocks.

This is **1 ten.**

Each block is one

Here are **5 ones.**

The number is 15.

1.
tens [ ]   ones [ ]
Write the number: [ ]

2.
tens [ ]   ones [ ]
Write the number: [ ]

3.
tens [ ]   ones [ ]
Write the number: [ ]

4.
tens [ ]   ones [ ]
Write the number: [ ]

5.
tens [ ]   ones [ ]
Write the number: [ ]

6.
tens [ ]   ones [ ]
Write the number: [ ]

7.
tens [ ]   ones [ ]
Write the number: [ ]

8.
tens [ ]   ones [ ]
Write the number: [ ]

9.
tens [ ]   ones [ ]
Write the number: [ ]

Canadian Math Basics Series  Grade 2

# Tens And Ones

**a.** Count the tens and ones. Write how many blocks in all.

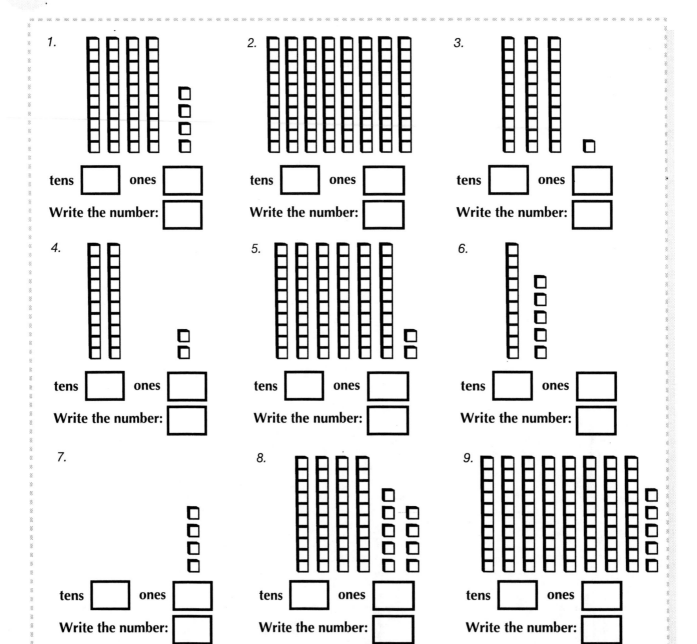

1.
tens ☐   ones ☐
Write the number: ☐

2.
tens ☐   ones ☐
Write the number: ☐

3.
tens ☐   ones ☐
Write the number: ☐

4.
tens ☐   ones ☐
Write the number: ☐

5.
tens ☐   ones ☐
Write the number: ☐

6.
tens ☐   ones ☐
Write the number: ☐

7.
tens ☐   ones ☐
Write the number: ☐

8.
tens ☐   ones ☐
Write the number: ☐

9.
tens ☐   ones ☐
Write the number: ☐

**b. Brain Stretch:** Circle the **larger** number in each set.

| 1. | 32 | 49 | 3. | 8 | 28 |
| 2. | 72 | 89 | 4. | 5 | 25 |

Chalkboard Publishing Inc © 2007              Canadian Math Basics Series  Grade 2

# Writing Numbers In Different Ways

a. Circle two correct ways to make each number.

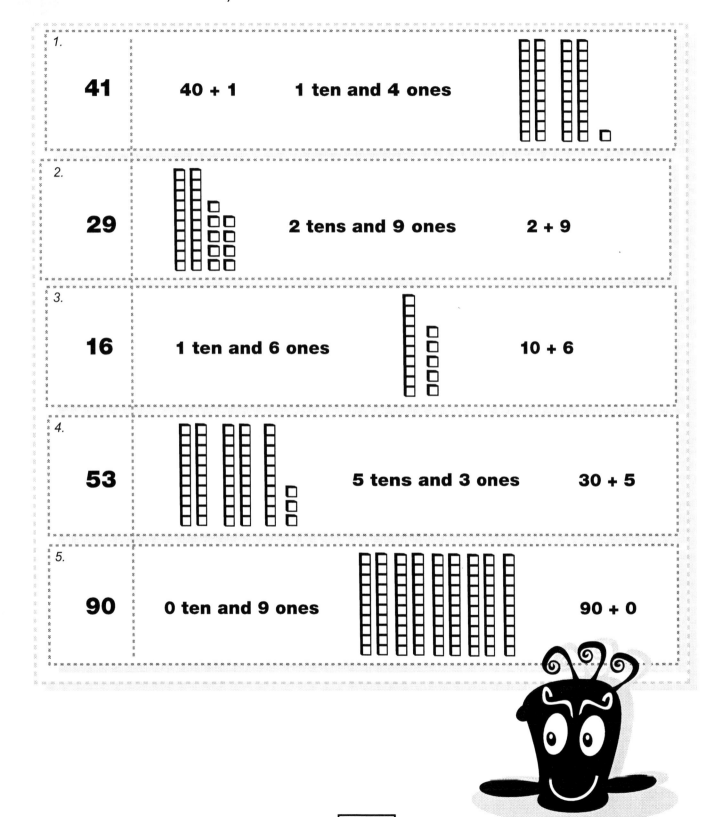

1. 41    40 + 1    1 ten and 4 ones

2. 29    2 tens and 9 ones    2 + 9

3. 16    1 ten and 6 ones    10 + 6

4. 53    5 tens and 3 ones    30 + 5

5. 90    0 ten and 9 ones    90 + 0

Chalkboard Publishing Inc © 2007

# Writing Numbers In Standard Form

**a.** Write each number in standard form.

> **Math Talk: Standard Form**
> Standard form are numbers written using digits.
> **For example: 30 + 5 = 35**
>
> **3 tens 5 ones = 35**

1. **40 + 5 =** _____

2. **seven tens  6 ones =** _____

3. **nineteen =** _____

4. **60 + 2 =** _____

5. **8 tens  4 ones =** _____

6. **eleven =** _____

7. **50 + 6 =** _____

8. **eight =** _____

9. **5 tens  3 ones =** _____

10. **four** _____

11. **3 tens  9 ones =** _____

12. **80 + 4 =** _____

Canadian Math Basics Series  Grade 2

# Sum Fun

**a.** Complete the sums and colour the spaces using the number key.

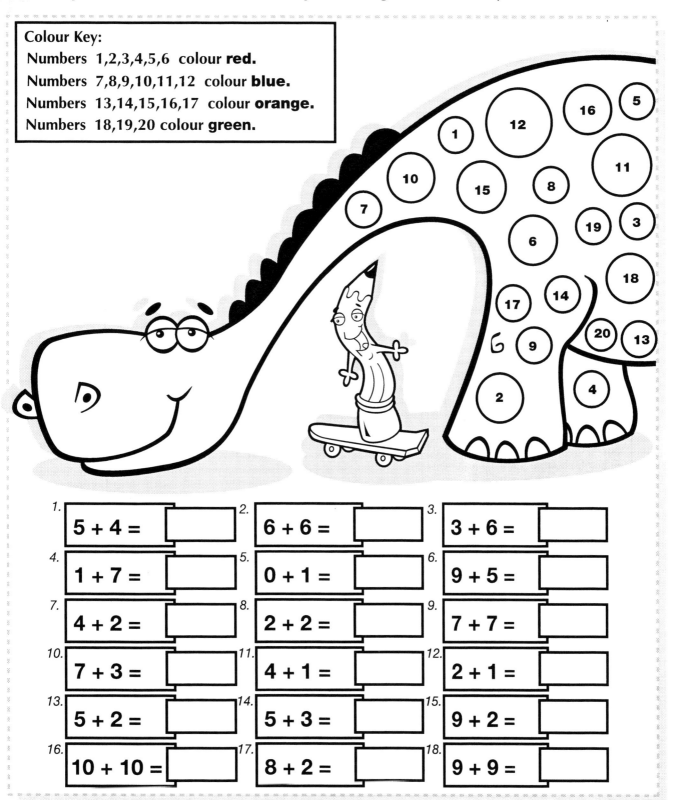

Colour Key:
Numbers 1,2,3,4,5,6 colour **red.**
Numbers 7,8,9,10,11,12 colour **blue.**
Numbers 13,14,15,16,17 colour **orange.**
Numbers 18,19,20 colour **green.**

1. 5 + 4 =

2. 6 + 6 =

3. 3 + 6 =

4. 1 + 7 =

5. 0 + 1 =

6. 9 + 5 =

7. 4 + 2 =

8. 2 + 2 =

9. 7 + 7 =

10. 7 + 3 =

11. 4 + 1 =

12. 2 + 1 =

13. 5 + 2 =

14. 5 + 3 =

15. 9 + 2 =

16. 10 + 10 =

17. 8 + 2 =

18. 9 + 9 =

Canadian Math Basics Series Grade 2

# Missing Numbers

**a. Fill in the missing numbers to complete the sums.**

1.  3
    + ☐
    ___
    6

2.  9
    + ☐
    ___
    18

3.  3
    + ☐
    ___
    12

4.  7
    + ☐
    ___
    12

5.  ☐
    + 7
    ___
    13

6.  6
    + ☐
    ___
    12

7.  9
    + ☐
    ___
    17

8.  ☐
    + 2
    ___
    11

9.  1
    + ☐
    ___
    11

10. 7
    + ☐
    ___
    7

11. ☐
    + 10
    ___
    20

12. ☐
    + 9
    ___
    14

13. 3
    + ☐
    ___
    5

14. 2
    + ☐
    ___
    6

15. 10
    + ☐
    ___
    15

16. ☐
    + 8
    ___
    16

17. 10
    + ☐
    ___
    20

18. ☐
    + 4
    ___
    10

Canadian Math Basics Series  Grade 2

# Addition Riddle

**a.** Complete the following math riddle.

*Why did the teacher wear sunglasses to school?*

| 10 + 10 = ☐ | **B** | 3 + 0 = ☐ | **Y** |
| 6 + 1 = ☐ | **T** | 2 + 6 = ☐ | **U** |
| 4 + 2 = ☐ | **E** | 8 + 5 = ☐ | **N** |
| 5 + 5 = ☐ | **D** | 7 + 9 = ☐ | **S** |
| 7 + 7 = ☐ | **W** | 8 + 10 = ☐ | **I** |
| 6 + 3 = ☐ | **C** | 2 + 9 = ☐ | **H** |
| 2 + 2 = ☐ | **G** | 10 + 7 = ☐ | **R** |
| 9 + 6 = ☐ | **L** | | |
| 4 + 8 = ☐ | **A** | | |

☐ ☐ ☐ ☐ ☐ ☐ ☐ | ☐ ☐ ☐ | ☐ ☐ ☐ ☐ ☐ ☐ ☐ ☐
20 6 9 12 8 16 6 | 11 6 17 | 16 7 8 10 6 13 7 16

☐ ☐ ☐ ☐ | ☐ ☐ ☐ ☐ ☐ ☐ | ☐ ☐ ☐ ☐ ☐ ☐
14 6 17 6 | 17 6 12 15 15 3 | 20 17 18 4 11 7 **!**

**b. Brain Stretch:** Complete the following.

1. **8 + 6 + 3 =** ☐     2. **5 + 9 + 0 =** ☐

3. **2 + 7 + 4 =** ☐     4. **1 + 8 + 3 =** ☐

Canadian Math Basics Series Grade 2

# Difference Fun

a. **Complete the sums and colour the spaces using the number key.**

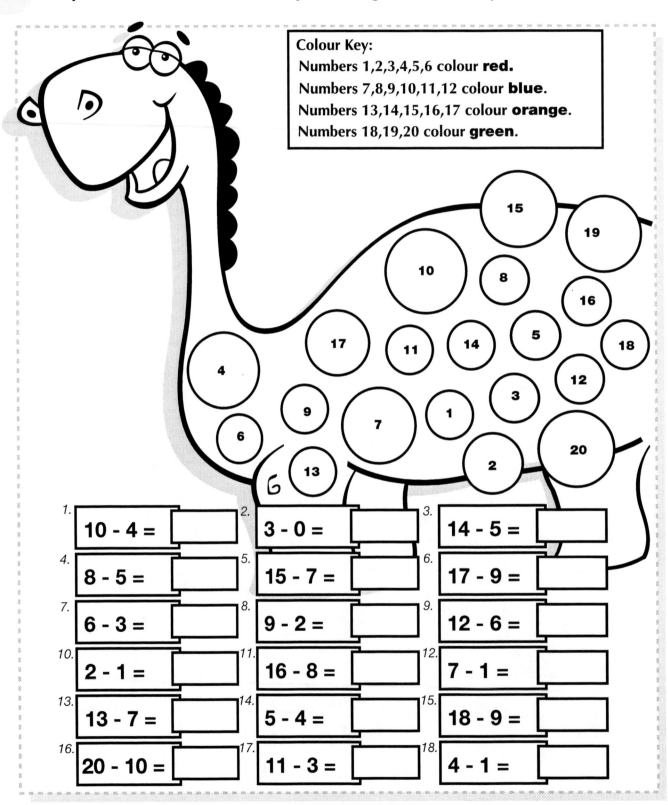

**Colour Key:**
Numbers 1,2,3,4,5,6 colour **red.**
Numbers 7,8,9,10,11,12 colour **blue.**
Numbers 13,14,15,16,17 colour **orange.**
Numbers 18,19,20 colour **green.**

1. 10 - 4 =

2. 3 - 0 =

3. 14 - 5 =

4. 8 - 5 =

5. 15 - 7 =

6. 17 - 9 =

7. 6 - 3 =

8. 9 - 2 =

9. 12 - 6 =

10. 2 - 1 =

11. 16 - 8 =

12. 7 - 1 =

13. 13 - 7 =

14. 5 - 4 =

15. 18 - 9 =

16. 20 - 10 =

17. 11 - 3 =

18. 4 - 1 =

Canadian Math Basics Series Grade 2

# Subtraction Practice

**a. Find the differences.**

1.
```
  12
-  3
```

2.
```
   6
-  2
```

3.
```
  20
- 10
```

4.
```
   4
-  0
```

5.
```
   8
-  3
```

6.
```
  17
-  9
```

7.
```
  11
-  3
```

8.
```
  14
-  8
```

9.
```
  16
-  9
```

10.
```
  10
-  2
```

11.
```
  15
-  6
```

12.
```
   7
-  0
```

13.
```
  18
-  8
```

14.
```
  13
-  6
```

15.
```
   5
-  4
```

16.
```
  12
-  6
```

17.
```
   8
-  2
```

18.
```
  16
-  9
```

Have a great day!

**b. Brain Stretch:** Use the numbers to write related facts.

1.    **8  6  2**

_____ + _____ = _____

_____ + _____ = _____

_____ - _____ = _____

_____ - _____ = _____

2.    **3  7  10**

_____ + _____ = _____

_____ + _____ = _____

_____ - _____ = _____

_____ - _____ = _____

Canadian Math Basics Series  Grade 2

# Subtraction Practice

## a. Find the differences.

1.
$$13 - 6$$

2.
$$12 - 8$$

3.
$$2 - 1$$

4.
$$8 - 0$$

5.
$$11 - 4$$

6.
$$17 - 10$$

7.
$$9 - 3$$

8.
$$6 - 2$$

9.
$$18 - 8$$

10.
$$20 - 10$$

11.
$$9 - 4$$

12.
$$11 - 8$$

13.
$$6 - 3$$

14.
$$15 - 7$$

15.
$$10 - 9$$

16.
$$4 - 3$$

17.
$$11 - 2$$

18.
$$3 - 2$$

## b. Brain Stretch:

1. 12 - 4 - 3 ☐

2. 18 - 9 - 5 ☐

3. 14 - 8 - 2 ☐

4. 17 - 2 - 6 ☐

Canadian Math Basics Series  Grade 2

# Missing Numbers

**a.** Fill in the missing numbers to complete the differences.

1.
```
   12
-  □
─────
    8
```

2.
```
    4
-   □
─────
    2
```

3.
```
   16
-   □
─────
    7
```

4.
```
    5
-   □
─────
    2
```

5.
```
    □
-   7
─────
    8
```

6.
```
    9
-   □
─────
    6
```

7.
```
    8
-   □
─────
    5
```

8.
```
    □
-   2
─────
    5
```

9.
```
    1
-   □
─────
    1
```

10.
```
   17
-   □
─────
    9
```

11.
```
    □
-  10
─────
   20
```

12.
```
    □
-   9
─────
    6
```

13.
```
   13
-   □
─────
    4
```

14.
```
   12
-   □
─────
    6
```

15.
```
   10
-   □
─────
    5
```

16.
```
    □
-  10
─────
    7
```

17.
```
    3
-   □
─────
    2
```

18.
```
    □
-   4
─────
   10
```

Canadian Math Basics Series  Grade 2

# Difference Riddle

**a.** Complete the following math riddle.

What kind of bow can you never tie?

16 - 8 = ☐   **R**

7 - 4 = ☐   **B**

10 - 8 = ☐   **I**

8 - 4 = ☐   **O**

6 - 1 = ☐   **N**

7 - 6 = ☐   **W**

13 - 7 = ☐   **A**

☐ | ☐ ☐ ☐ ☐ ☐ ☐ ☐ **!**

6   8   6   2   5   3   4   1

**b. Brain Stretch:** Match the numbers to the words.

sixteen  •     •  9

four  •     •  18

twelve  •     •  16

nine  •     •  12

eighteen  •     •  4

# Story Problems

**a.** Write an addition or subtraction sentence to solve each word problem.

1. Dave had **11** boxes of crayons. He gave **5** of them to his friends. How many boxes of crayons are left?

_____ ◯ _____ = ☐

2. Abby had **12** cookies. She gave **8** cookies to her sister. How many cookies does Abby have left?

_____ ◯ _____ = ☐

3. Val bought **6** daisies and **9** tulips. How many flowers did she buy in all?

_____ ◯ _____ = ☐

4. Nicole has **18** jelly beans. She gives **8** jelly beans to Sam. How many jelly beans does Nicole have left?

_____ ◯ _____ = ☐

5. Bob has **12** pieces of bubble gum. He gave **5** pieces of bubble gum to Sally. How many pieces does he have left?

_____ ◯ _____ = ☐

6. Marci has **3** cats and **7** hamsters. How many pets does she have altogether?

_____ ◯ _____ = ☐

7. Jim has **14** baseball cards. He gave **5** to Nicole. How many does Jim have left?

_____ ◯ _____ = ☐

**b. Brain Stretch:** Fill in the missing numbers.

1.
$$\begin{array}{r} 10 \\ + \ \square \\ \hline 15 \end{array}$$

2.
$$\begin{array}{r} \square \\ - \ 5 \\ \hline 10 \end{array}$$

3.
$$\begin{array}{r} 9 \\ + \ \square \\ \hline 15 \end{array}$$

4.
$$\begin{array}{r} \square \\ - \ 5 \\ \hline 9 \end{array}$$

5.
$$\begin{array}{r} \square \\ - \ 7 \\ \hline 4 \end{array}$$

Canadian Math Basics Series  Grade 2

# Add Or Subtract

**a.** Use the number line to find the sum or difference.

> **Math Talk:**
>
> To find the sum of two numbers count forward.
>
> **For example: 14 + 5 = 19   ( 14,15,16,17,18,19 )**
>
> To find the diference of two numbers count backward.
>
> **For example: 29 - 4 = 25   ( 29,28,27,26,25 )**

0 1 2 3 4 5 6 7 8 9 10 11 12 13 14 15 16 17 18 19 20 21 22 23 24 25 26 27 28 29 30

1.   26 + 3 =

2.   17 + 2 =

3.   16 - 5 =

4.   27 - 5 =

5.   18 + 9 =

6.   18 + 2 =

7.   16 - 3 =

8.   29 - 8 =

9.   22 + 6 =

10.   16 + 5 =

11.   30 - 5 =

12.   19 - 1 =

13.   18 + 7 =

14.   15 + 7 =

15.   11 - 4 =

16.   28 - 9 =

Canadian Math Basics Series  Grade 2

# Two Digit Addition Without Regrouping

**a.** Solve the sums.

> **Math Talk: Two Digit Addition**
> Always line up the ones and tens columns when adding.
>
> **Add the ones column first.**       **Then add the tens column**
>
> tens / ones                                    tens / ones
>
>     2 | 3                                           2 | 3
> +   4 | 5                                       +   4 | 5
> ---------                                       ---------
>         | 8                                          6 | 8

1.
```
   54
+  31
------
```

2.
```
   22
+  15
------
```

3.
```
   71
+  27
------
```

4.
```
   35
+  62
------
```

5.
```
   44
+  30
------
```

6.
```
   12
+  50
------
```

7.
```
   76
+  12
------
```

8.
```
   62
+  23
------
```

9.
```
   84
+  11
------
```

10.
```
   33
+  13
------
```

11.
```
   54
+  33
------
```

12.
```
   31
+  26
------
```

13.
```
   53
+  11
------
```

14.
```
   62
+  37
------
```

15.
```
   14
+  30
------
```

16.
```
   82
+  15
------
```

17.
```
   12
+  40
------
```

18.
```
   34
+  14
------
```

19.
```
   20
+  13
------
```

20.
```
   52
+  43
------
```

Canadian Math Basics Series  Grade 2

# Addition Riddle

a. Complete the following math riddle.

Why did the dog say "meow?"

| 62   I | 32   R | 18   W | 81   L |
|---|---|---|---|
| + 35 | + 10 | + 60 | + 11 |

| 12   H | 71   T | 52   V | 31   U |
|---|---|---|---|
| + 13 | + 14 | + 21 | + 34 |

| 21   G | 31   X | 43   E | 43   O |
|---|---|---|---|
| + 11 | + 40 | + 41 | + 31 |

| 44   A | 45   B | 32   S | 21   N |
|---|---|---|---|
| + 22 | + 51 | + 27 | + 32 |

25  84 | 78  66  59 | 92  84  66  42  53  97  53  32 | 66 | 53  84  78 |

92  66  53  32  65  66  32  84  !

# Two Digit Addition With Regrouping

**a.** Find the following sums.

| **Math Talk: Two Digit Addition** | **example:** |
|---|---|
| | tens / ones |
| 1. Always line up the ones and then the tens columns. | 1 |
| | 2 \| 6 |
| 2. Add the ones column first, then add the tens column. | + 2 \| 6 |
| | 5 \| 2 |
| 3. When the sum of the ones column is **greater** than 9, regroup the ones and carry it over to the tens column. | carry the one from 12 to the tens column. |

1.
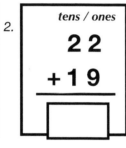

tens / ones

```
  6 4
+ 1 8
```

2.
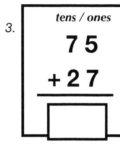

tens / ones

```
  2 2
+ 1 9
```

3.
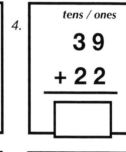

tens / ones

```
  7 5
+ 2 7
```

4.
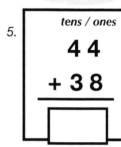

tens / ones

```
  3 9
+ 2 2
```

5.

tens / ones

```
  4 4
+ 3 8
```

6.
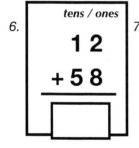

tens / ones

```
  1 2
+ 5 8
```

7.
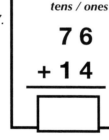

tens / ones

```
  7 6
+ 1 4
```

8.
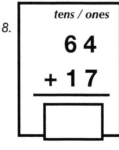

tens / ones

```
  6 4
+ 1 7
```

9.
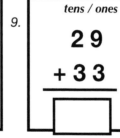

tens / ones

```
  2 9
+ 3 3
```

10.

tens / ones

```
  3 6
+ 3 6
```

11.
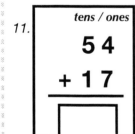

tens / ones

```
  5 4
+ 1 7
```

12.
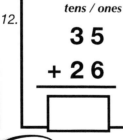

tens / ones

```
  3 5
+ 2 6
```

13.
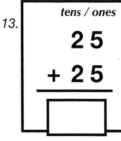

tens / ones

```
  2 5
+ 2 5
```

14.
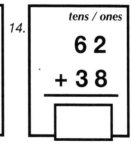

tens / ones

```
  6 2
+ 3 8
```

15.

tens / ones

```
  1 7
+ 2 7
```

23

# Sum It Up

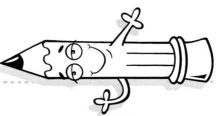

**a.** Solve the sums.

1.
```
tens / ones
   2 6
 + 4 5
```

2.
```
tens / ones
   6 7
 + 1 7
```

3.
```
tens / ones
   2 5
 + 6 9
```

4.
```
tens / ones
   2 5
 + 1 5
```

5.
```
tens / ones
   1 6
 + 5 8
```

6.
```
tens / ones
   3 9
 + 3 4
```

7.
```
tens / ones
   7 1
 + 1 9
```

8.
```
tens / ones
   1 6
 + 6 6
```

9.
```
tens / ones
   3 8
 + 2 7
```

10.
```
tens / ones
   6 5
 + 1 6
```

11.
```
tens / ones
   2 6
 + 5 6
```

12.
```
tens / ones
   3 4
 + 4 8
```

13.
```
tens / ones
   4 3
 + 2 9
```

14.
```
tens / ones
   2 2
 + 6 9
```

15.
```
tens / ones
   7 8
 + 1 8
```

**b.** **Brain Stretch:** Write an addition sentence and multiplication sentence for each of the following.

*1.* **4 rows of 5**

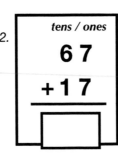

4 x 5 = ☐

___ + ___ + ___ + ___ = ☐

*2.* **3 rows of 3**

3 x 3 = ☐

___ + ___ + ___ = ☐

Chalkboard Publishing Inc © 2007

Canadian Math Basics Series  Grade 2

# 2 Digit Subtraction Without Regrouping

a. Solve.

**Math Talk: Two Digit Subtraction**

Always line up the ones and tens columns when subtracting.

**Subtract the ones column first.**

tens / ones

```
  8 | 7
- 4 | 4
    | 3
```

**Then subtract the tens column.**

tens / ones

```
  8 | 7
- 4 | 4
  4 | 3
```

1.
```
  58
- 13
```

2.
```
  87
- 43
```

3.
```
  29
- 13
```

4.
```
  74
- 30
```

5.
```
  36
- 12
```

6.
```
  78
- 23
```

7.
```
  96
- 32
```

8.
```
  84
- 72
```

9.
```
  67
- 23
```

10.
```
  85
- 14
```

11.
```
  49
- 27
```

12.
```
  67
- 41
```

13.
```
  25
- 15
```

14.
```
  46
- 35
```

15.
```
  36
- 16
```

16.
```
  86
- 31
```

17.
```
  43
- 41
```

18.
```
  98
- 23
```

19.
```
  72
- 21
```

20.
```
  32
- 30
```

# Subtraction Match

**a. Match the following.**

1.
$$45 - 31$$

2.
$$96 - 52$$

3.
$$97 - 30$$

4.
$$28 - 12$$

5.
$$73 - 22$$

6.
$$38 - 35$$

7.
$$79 - 48$$

8.
$$84 - 62$$

9.
$$59 - 25$$

10.
$$67 - 56$$

11.
$$78 - 50$$

67

3

31

22

16

14

11

44

28

51

34

# Subtraction With Regrouping

a. Find the differences.

**Math Talk: Subtraction With Regrouping**

1. Subtract the ones column first, then subtract the tens column.

2. When the bottom number of the ones column in the equation is **greater** than the top number, borrow a group of **10** from the tens column.

**example:**
tens / ones

```
  3   1
  4 | 2
- 3 | 9
  ----
      3
```

You can't take 9 away from 2, so borrow a group of 10 from the 4.

---

1.
```
tens / ones
   6 1
 - 2 5
 -----
```

2.
```
tens / ones
   7 3
 - 1 6
 -----
```

3.
```
tens / ones
   6 1
 - 2 4
 -----
```

4.
```
tens / ones
   4 2
 - 3 3
 -----
```

5.
```
tens / ones
   2 4
 - 1 7
 -----
```

6.
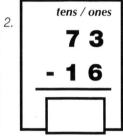
```
tens / ones
   3 5
 - 1 8
 -----
```

7.
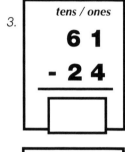
```
tens / ones
   5 2
 - 2 5
 -----
```

8.
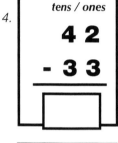
```
tens / ones
   7 1
 - 5 4
 -----
```

9.
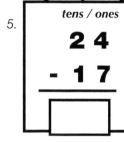
```
tens / ones
   6 3
 - 2 7
 -----
```

10.
```
tens / ones
   3 1
 - 1 2
 -----
```

11.
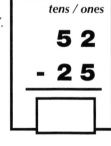
```
tens / ones
   5 4
 - 4 6
 -----
```

12.
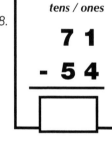
```
tens / ones
   8 3
 - 2 6
 -----
```

13.
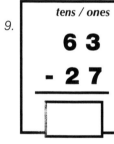
```
tens / ones
   9 2
 - 7 5
 -----
```

14.
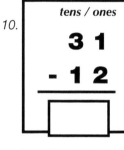
```
tens / ones
   7 1
 - 1 3
 -----
```

15.
```
tens / ones
   4 0
 - 2 9
 -----
```

16.
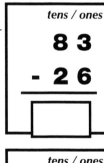
```
tens / ones
   5 1
 - 3 8
 -----
```

17.
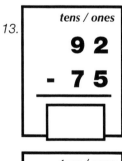
```
tens / ones
   6 7
 - 4 8
 -----
```

18.
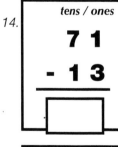
```
tens / ones
   4 1
 - 3 4
 -----
```

19.
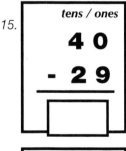
```
tens / ones
   9 2
 - 5 6
 -----
```

20.
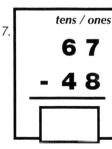
```
tens / ones
   4 2
 - 2 4
 -----
```

Canadian Math Basics Series  Grade 2

# Subtraction Riddle

a. Complete the following math riddle.

When do you hear a computer make a squeak noise?

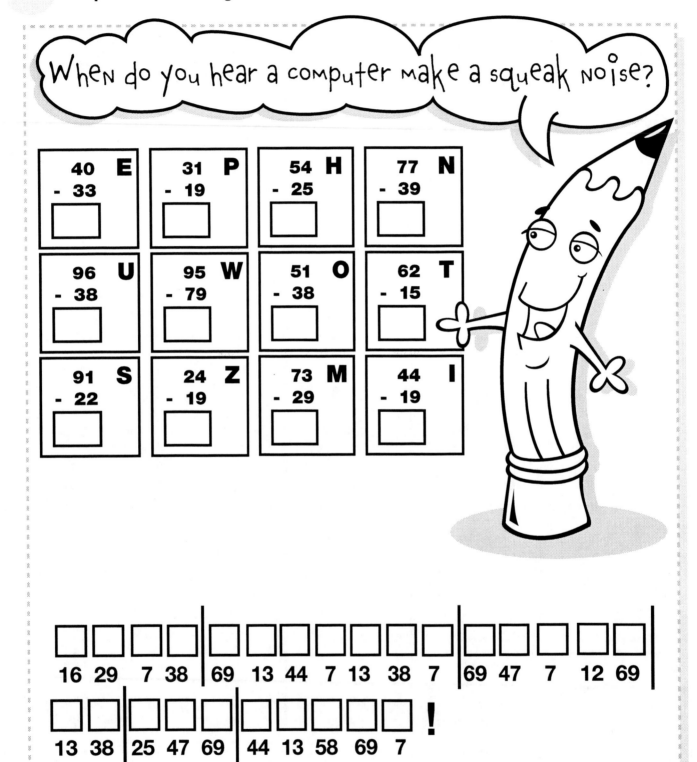

| | | | |
|---|---|---|---|
| 40  E<br>- 33 | 31  P<br>- 19 | 54  H<br>- 25 | 77  N<br>- 39 |
| 96  U<br>- 38 | 95  W<br>- 79 | 51  O<br>- 38 | 62  T<br>- 15 |
| 91  S<br>- 22 | 24  Z<br>- 19 | 73  M<br>- 29 | 44  I<br>- 19 |

☐ ☐ ☐ ☐ | ☐ ☐ ☐ ☐ ☐ ☐ ☐ | ☐ ☐ ☐ ☐ ☐
16 29 7 38 | 69 13 44 7 13 38 7 | 69 47 7 12 69

☐ ☐ | ☐ ☐ ☐ | ☐ ☐ ☐ ☐ ☐ !
13 38 | 25 47 69 | 44 13 58 69 7

Canadian Math Basics Series  Grade 2

# Word Problems

**a.** Complete the following word problems.

| Word Problems | Show Your Work |
|---|---|

**1.** Paul had **23** blue marbles and **39** red marbles. How many marbles are there altogether?

There are _____ marbles.

**2.** There are **41** birds in the tree. **23** birds flew away. How many birds are left in the tree?

_____ birds are left.

**3.** There were **82** jelly beans in the jar. David ate **36** of them. How many jelly beans were left?

There are _____ jelly beans left.

**4.** Katie has **38** green buttons and **28** blue buttons. How many buttons does she have in all?

There are _____ buttons in all.

Chalkboard Publishing Inc © 2007

Canadian Math Basics Series  Grade 2

# Introduction To Multiplication

**a.** Complete the addition sentence and multiplication sentence for each of the following.

---

**Math Talk: Introduction To Multiplication**

| Look at the groups of 3. | Addition Sentence | Multiplication Sentence |
|---|---|---|
| | There are 3 equal groups of germs. | There are 3 groups of 3. |
| | 3 + 3 + 3 = 9 | 3 x 3 = 9 |

---

1.

**6 + 6 =**                                       **2 x 6 =**

2.

**2 + 2 + 2 =**                                   **3 x 2 =**

3.

**10 + 10 =**                                     **2 x 10 =**

4.

**3 + 3 + 3 + 3 =**                               **4 x 3 =**

5.

**7 + 7 =**                                       **2 x 7 =**

6.

**8 + 8 =**                                       **2 x 8 =**

Chalkboard Publishing Inc © 2007

Canadian Math Basics Series Grade 2

# Introduction To Multiplication

**a.** Complete the addition sentence and multiplication sentence for each of the following.

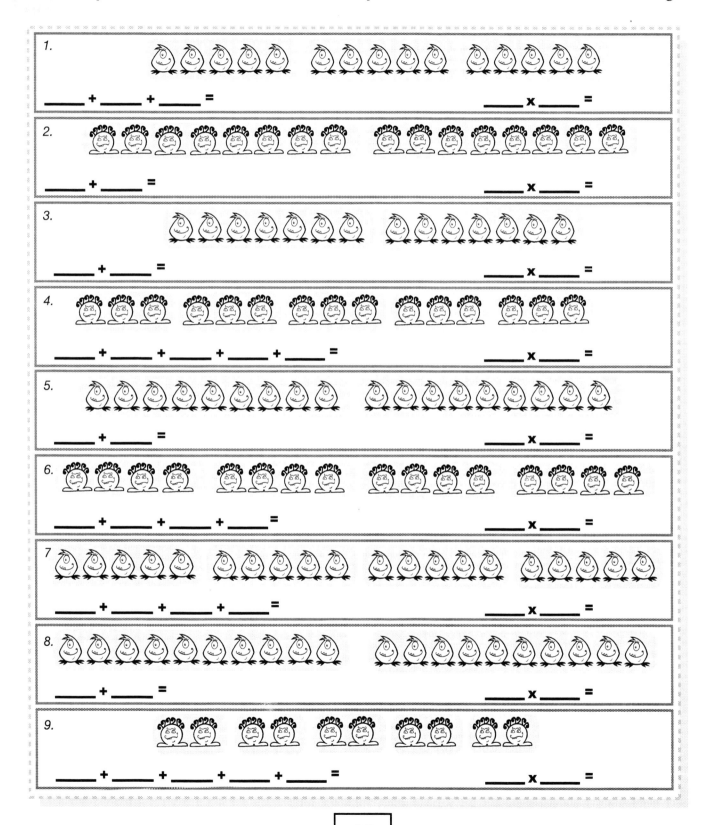

1.

_____ + _____ + _____ =                    _____ x _____ =

2.

_____ + _____ =                    _____ x _____ =

3.

_____ + _____ =                    _____ x _____ =

4.

_____ + _____ + _____ + _____ + _____ =                    _____ x _____ =

5.

_____ + _____ =                    _____ x _____ =

6.

_____ + _____ + _____ + _____ =                    _____ x _____ =

7

_____ + _____ + _____ + _____ =                    _____ x _____ =

8.

_____ + _____ =                    _____ x _____ =

9.

_____ + _____ + _____ + _____ + _____ =                    _____ x _____ =

31

# Skip Counting

**a.** Fill in the missing numbers.

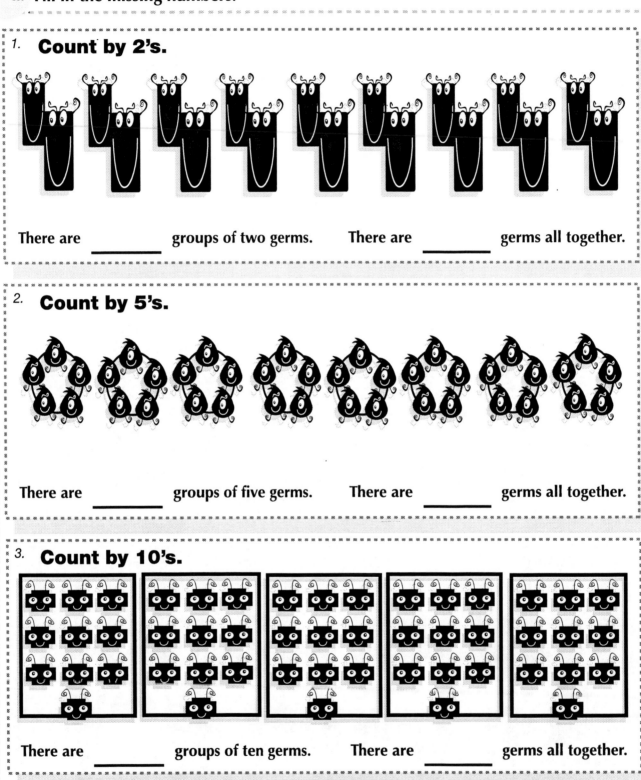

*1.* **Count by 2's.**

There are _____ groups of two germs.    There are _____ germs all together.

*2.* **Count by 5's.**

There are _____ groups of five germs.    There are _____ germs all together.

*3.* **Count by 10's.**

There are _____ groups of ten germs.    There are _____ germs all together.

Canadian Math Basics Series  Grade 2

# Fractions: Equal Parts

**a.** Find the shapes that show halves. Colour 1/2.

**Math Talk: Fractions Have Equal Parts**

The square is divided into 2 equal parts.
This means that 1 out of 2 parts is shaded.

$$\frac{1}{2}$$  how many parts / total parts

One half is shaded.

1.

2.

3.

4.

5.

6.

7.

Canadian Math Basics Series  Grade 2

# Exploring Fractions

**a.** What fraction does the coloured part show? Circle the fraction.

**Math Talk:** Fractions show equal parts of a whole.

This means 1 out of 3 equal parts is shaded.

$$\frac{1}{3}\quad\begin{array}{l}\text{how many parts}\\ \text{total parts}\end{array}$$

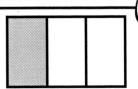

One third is shaded.

| 1. | 2. | 3. |
|---|---|---|
|  |  |  |
| $\frac{1}{2}$  $\frac{1}{3}$  $\frac{1}{4}$ | $\frac{1}{2}$  $\frac{1}{3}$  $\frac{1}{4}$ | $\frac{1}{2}$  $\frac{1}{3}$  $\frac{1}{4}$ |

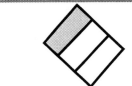

| 4. | 5. | 6. |
|---|---|---|
|  | 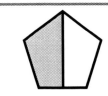 |  |
| $\frac{1}{2}$  $\frac{1}{3}$  $\frac{1}{4}$ | $\frac{1}{2}$  $\frac{1}{3}$  $\frac{1}{4}$ | $\frac{1}{2}$  $\frac{1}{3}$  $\frac{1}{4}$ |

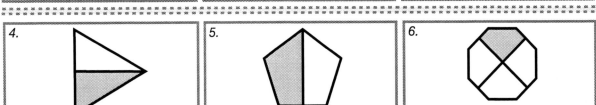

| 7. | 8. | 9. |
|---|---|---|
|  | 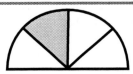 | 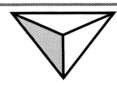 |
| $\frac{1}{2}$  $\frac{1}{3}$  $\frac{1}{4}$ | $\frac{1}{2}$  $\frac{1}{3}$  $\frac{1}{4}$ | $\frac{1}{2}$  $\frac{1}{3}$  $\frac{1}{4}$ |

| 10. | 11. | 12. |
|---|---|---|
|  | 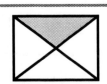 | 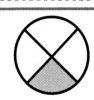 |
| $\frac{1}{2}$  $\frac{1}{3}$  $\frac{1}{4}$ | $\frac{1}{2}$  $\frac{1}{3}$  $\frac{1}{4}$ | $\frac{1}{2}$  $\frac{1}{3}$  $\frac{1}{4}$ |

Canadian Math Basics Series  Grade 2

# Exploring Fractions

**a.** Write a fraction to show how much of the shape is shaded.

1.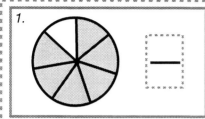

2.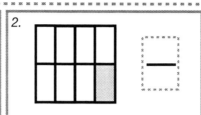

3.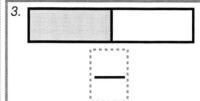

4.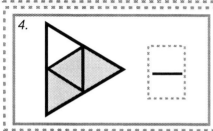

5.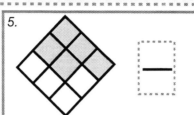

6.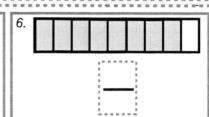

7.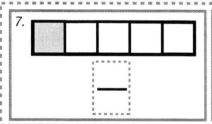

8.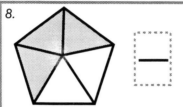

9.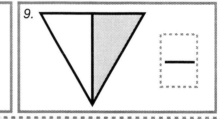

10.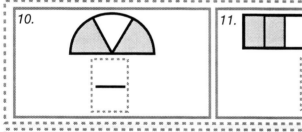

11.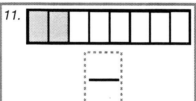

12.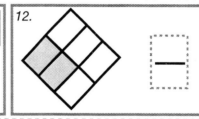

13.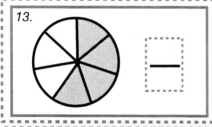

14.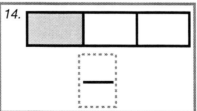

15.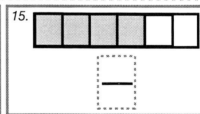

16.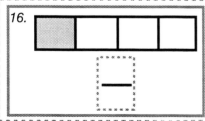

17.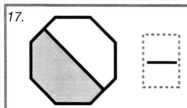

18.

Canadian Math Basics Series Grade 2

# Exploring Fractions

**a.** Write a fraction to show how much of the shape is shaded.

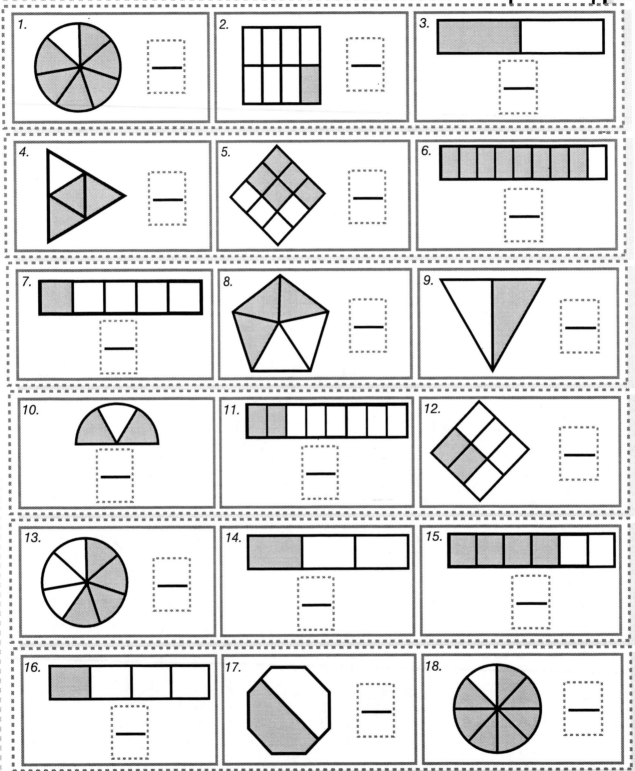

Canadian Math Basics Series  Grade 2

# Fractions As Part Of A Group

a. Complete.

1. Colour $\frac{1}{4}$

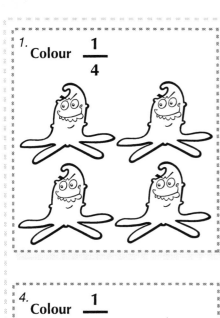

2. Colour $\frac{1}{2}$

3. Colour $\frac{1}{4}$

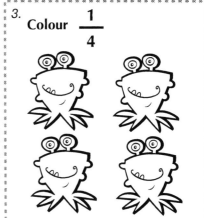

4. Colour $\frac{1}{3}$

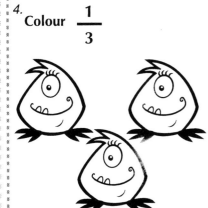

5. Colour $\frac{1}{2}$

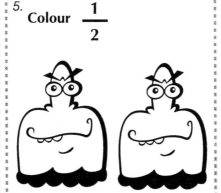

6. Colour $\frac{1}{3}$

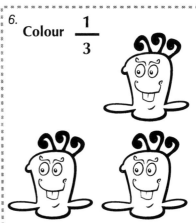

7. Colour $\frac{1}{4}$

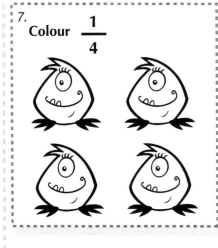

8. Colour $\frac{1}{3}$

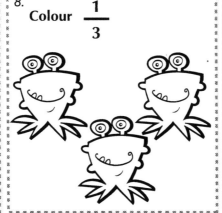

9. Colour $\frac{1}{2}$

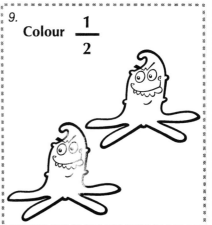

Canadian Math Basics Series  Grade 2

# Fraction Problems

**a.** Show how you could share the following.

1. Alex cut a pizza into **fourths**. How many friends could Alex share it with? Draw a picture and show your answer in a fraction.

2. Megan has **two old sweaters** and **one new sweater**. What fraction of Megan's sweaters are **old**? Draw a picture and show your answer as a fraction.

3. Kaitlyn has **4 pieces** of chocolate. She gives her friend half of the chocolate. How many pieces did she give her friend?

4. Madelyn has **4 pieces** of bubble gum. She gives **3 pieces away**. What is the fraction she gave away? Draw a picture and show your answer as a fraction.

5. David has **two cookies**. He gives **a cookie** to his friend Barney. How many cookies will each person get? Draw a picture and show your answer as a fraction.

Canadian Math Basics Series  Grade 2

# Telling Time To The Hour

**a.** Write the time two ways.

1.

_____ o' clock

_____ : _____

2.

_____ o' clock

_____ : _____

3.

_____ o' clock

_____ : _____

4.

_____ o' clock

_____ : _____

5.

_____ o' clock

_____ : _____

6.
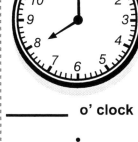

_____ o' clock

_____ : _____

7.

_____ o' clock

_____ : _____

8.

_____ o' clock

_____ : _____

9.

_____ o' clock

_____ : _____

10.

_____ o' clock

_____ : _____

11.

_____ o' clock

_____ : _____

12.

_____ o' clock

_____ : _____

Canadian Math Basics Series  Grade 2

# Telling Time To The Half-Hour

**a.** Write the time in two ways.

| Math Talk: | The minute hand points to **6**. The hour hand is after the **3** but not quite at the **4**. |
|---|---|

The time is 3:30 or half past **3**.

1.

half past _____

_____ : _____

2.

half past _____

_____ : _____

3.

half past _____

_____ : _____

4.

half past _____

_____ : _____

5.

half past _____

_____ : _____

6.

half past _____

_____ : _____

7.

half past _____

_____ : _____

8.

half past _____

_____ : _____

9.

half past _____

_____ : _____

10.

half past _____

_____ : _____

11.

half past _____

_____ : _____

12.

half past _____

_____ : _____

Chalkboard Publishing Inc © 2007

Canadian Math Basics Series  Grade 2

# Telling Time To The Quarter Past

**a.** Write the time two ways.

**Math Talk:** The hour hand points just after **8**.
The minute hand points to the **3**

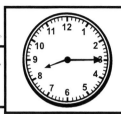

The time is 8:15 or
quarter past 8.

1.

quarter past _____

_____ : _____

2.

quarter past _____

_____ : _____

3.

quarter past _____

_____ : _____

4.

quarter past _____

_____ : _____

5.

quarter past _____

_____ : _____

6.

quarter past _____

_____ : _____

7.
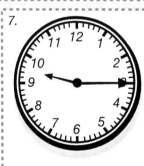

quarter past _____

_____ : _____

8.

quarter past _____

_____ : _____

9.

quarter past _____

_____ : _____

10.

quarter past _____

_____ : _____

11.

quarter past _____

_____ : _____

12.

quarter past _____

_____ : _____

Canadian Math Basics Series  Grade 2

# Telling Time To The Quarter Hour

**a.** Write the time two ways.

| **Math Talk:** | The minute hand points to **9**. The hour hand is after the **7** and almost at the **8**, but not quite. |
|---|---|

The time is 7:45 or quarter to 8.

1.

quarter to _____

_____ : _____

2.

quarter to _____

_____ : _____

3.

quarter to _____

_____ : _____

4.

quarter to _____

_____ : _____

5.

quarter to _____

_____ : _____

6.

quarter to _____

_____ : _____

7.

quarter to _____

_____ : _____

8.

quarter to _____

_____ : _____

9.

quarter to _____

_____ : _____

10.

quarter to _____

_____ : _____

11.

quarter to _____

_____ : _____

12.

quarter to _____

_____ : _____

Canadian Math Basics Series  Grade 2

# What Time Is It?

**a. Circle the correct time.**

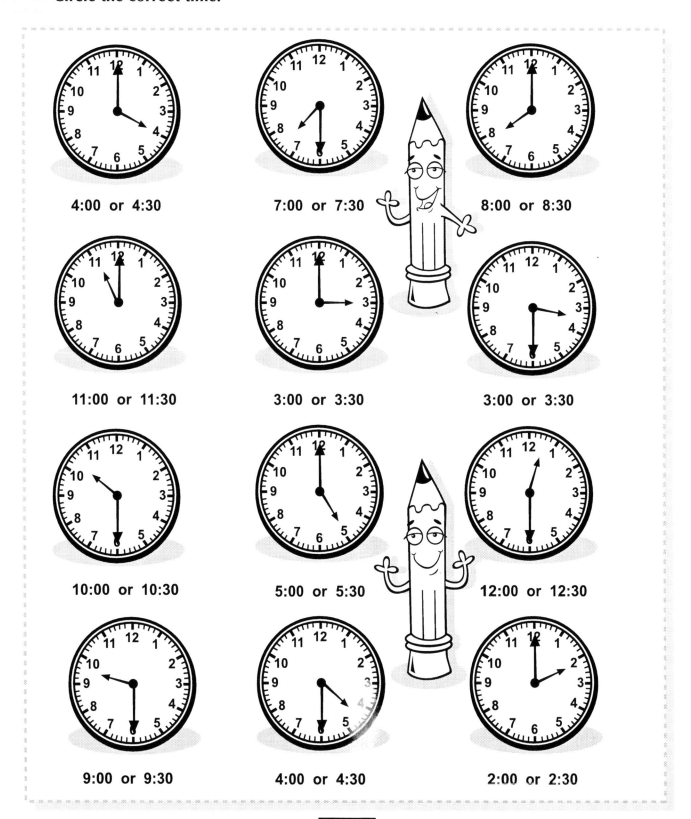

4:00 or 4:30          7:00 or 7:30          8:00 or 8:30

11:00 or 11:30          3:00 or 3:30          3:00 or 3:30

10:00 or 10:30          5:00 or 5:30          12:00 or 12:30

9:00 or 9:30          4:00 or 4:30          2:00 or 2:30

Chalkboard Publishing Inc © 2007                    Canadian Math Basics Series  Grade 2

# Show The Time

a. Draw the two hands on the clock to show the time.

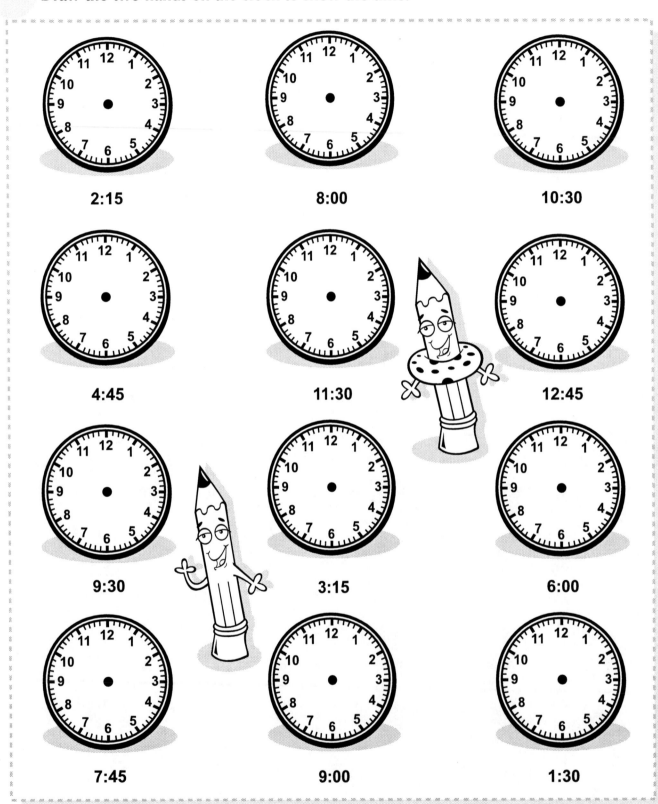

| | | |
|---|---|---|
| 2:15 | 8:00 | 10:30 |
| 4:45 | 11:30 | 12:45 |
| 9:30 | 3:15 | 6:00 |
| 7:45 | 9:00 | 1:30 |

Canadian Math Basics Series  Grade 2

# Calendar Time

**a.** Write the months of the year in order.

## Months of the Year

1. _____

2. _____

3. _____

4. _____

5. _____

6. _____

7. _____

8. _____

9. _____

10. _____

11. _____

12. _____

**May**

**September**

**December**

**February**

**August**

**April**

**July**

**March**

**October**

**June**

**November**

**January**

How many months in a year? _____

What is the month after July? _____

What month is your birthday? _____

Chalkboard Publishing Inc © 2007

Canadian Math Basics Series  Grade 2

# Reading A Calendar

**a.** Use the calendar to answer the questions.

## April

| Sunday | Monday | Tuesday | Wednesday | Thursday | Friday | Saturday |
|--------|--------|---------|-----------|----------|--------|----------|
|        |        | 1       | 2         | 3        | 4      | 5        |
| 6      | 7      | 8       | 9         | 10       | 11     | 12       |
| 13     | 14     | 15      | 16        | 17       | 18     | 19       |
| 20     | 21     | 22      | 23        | 24       | 25     | 26       |
| 27     | 28     | 29      | 30        |          |        |          |

1. What day of the week is **April 10**?

_____

2. How many **Tuesdays** are there?

_____

3. How many **Saturdays** are there?

_____

4. What is the date of the first **Monday**?

_____

5. What is the date of the **third Friday**?

_____

6. What day of the week is **April 5**?

_____

## September

| Sunday | Monday | Tuesday | Wednesday | Thursday | Friday | Saturday |
|--------|--------|---------|-----------|----------|--------|----------|
|        |        | 1       | 2         | 3        | 4      | 5        |
| 7      | 8      | 9       | 10        | 11       | 12     | 13       |
| 14     | 15     | 16      | 17        | 18       | 19     | 20       |
| 21     | 22     | 23      | 24        | 25       | 26     | 27       |
| 28     | 29     | 30      | 31        |          |        |          |

1. How many **days** are there in the month?

_____

2. What day of the week is **September 12**?

_____

3. On what day of the week will **next month** begin?

_____

4. How many **Fridays** are there?

_____

Canadian Math Basics Series  Grade 2

# Elapsed Time

**a.** Complete the times. Then write how long each lesson takes.

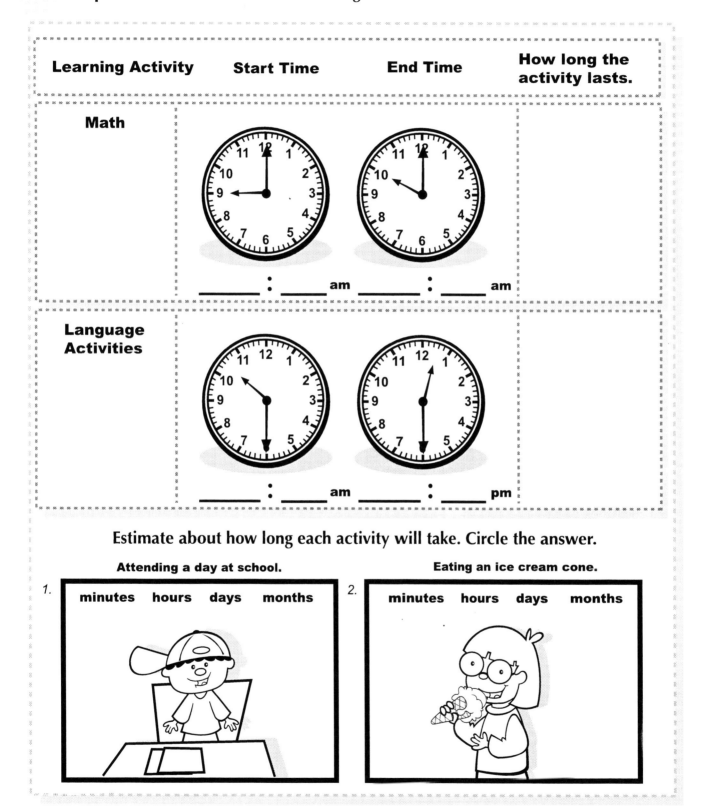

| Learning Activity | Start Time | End Time | How long the activity lasts. |
|---|---|---|---|
| Math | ____ : ____ am | ____ : ____ am | |
| Language Activities | ____ : ____ am | ____ : ____ pm | |

Estimate about how long each activity will take. Circle the answer.

**Attending a day at school.**

1.  minutes   hours   days   months

**Eating an ice cream cone.**

2.  minutes   hours   days   months

Canadian Math Basics Series  Grade 2

# Exploring Money

**a.** Write the name and the value of each of the following coins.

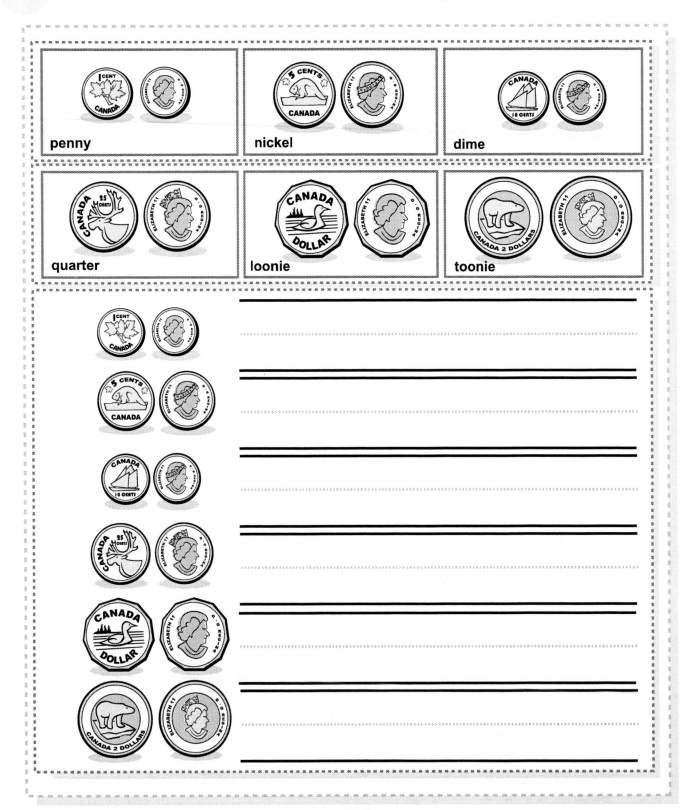

penny

nickel

dime

quarter

loonie

toonie

# Money Match

a. Match the items with the money prices.

**Price Tag $ 1.00** •

**Price Tag $ 0.51** •

**Price Tag $ 0.81** •

**Price Tag $ 0.56** •

**Price Tag $ 0.37** •

Canadian Math Basics Series  Grade 2

# Money Match

**a.** Match the items with the money prices.

**Price Tag $2.05**

**Price Tag $1.45**

**Price Tag $1.01**

**Price Tag $0.50**

**Price Tag $0.62**

Chalkboard Publishing Inc © 2007

Canadian Math Basics Series  Grade 2

# How Much Money?

**a.** Calculate how much money each person has. The first one is done for you.

1. **Spencer**

**Total**

$ 0.10    $ 0.25    $ 0.25    $ 0.10    $ 0.05      $ 0.75

2. **Ben**

$___.___   $___.___   $___.___   $___.___   $___.___    $___.___

3. **Carolyn**

$___.___   $___.___   $___.___   $___.___   $___.___    $___.___

4. **Mary**

$___.___   $___.___   $___.___   $___.___   $___.___    $___.___

5. Which person has the **most** money? _____

6. Which person has the **least** money? _____

Chalkboard Publishing Inc © 2007      Canadian Math Basics Series Grade 2

# How Much Money?

**a.** Calculate how much money each person has.

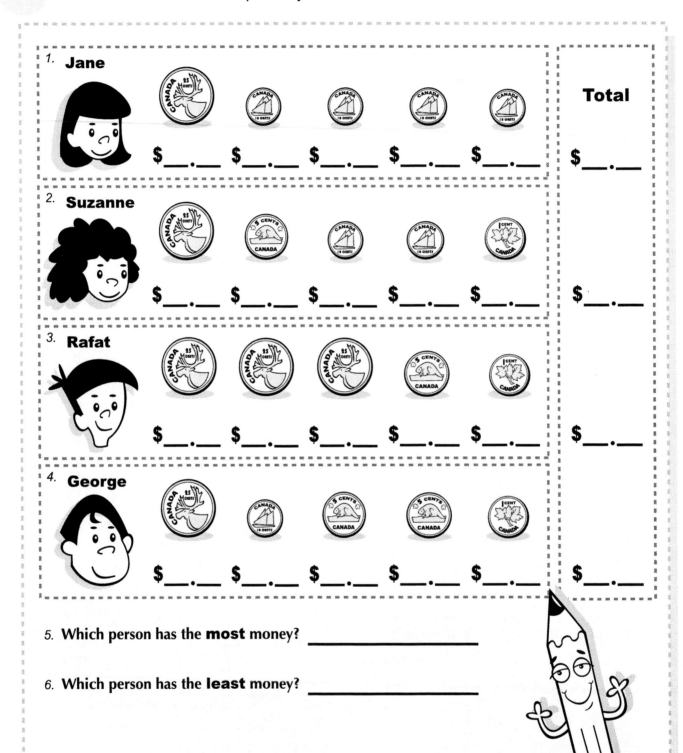

1. **Jane**

$____.____  $____.____  $____.____  $____.____  $____.____

**Total**

$____.____

2. **Suzanne**

$____.____  $____.____  $____.____  $____.____  $____.____

$____.____

3. **Rafat**

$____.____  $____.____  $____.____  $____.____  $____.____

$____.____

4. **George**

$____.____  $____.____  $____.____  $____.____  $____.____

$____.____

5. Which person has the **most** money? _____

6. Which person has the **least** money? _____

**Chalkboard Publishing Inc © 2007**

**Canadian Math Basics Series  Grade 2**

# Money

**a.** **Make money two ways.**

1.
[ ] pennies [ ] quarters  **$0.32**  [ ] pennies [ ] quarters
[ ] nickels [ ] dimes            [ ] nickels [ ] dimes

2.
[ ] pennies [ ] quarters  **$0.56**  [ ] pennies [ ] quarters
[ ] nickels [ ] dimes            [ ] nickels [ ] dimes

3.
[ ] pennies [ ] quarters  **$0.89**  [ ] pennies [ ] quarters
[ ] nickels [ ] dimes            [ ] nickels [ ] dimes

4.
[ ] pennies [ ] quarters  **$0.48**  [ ] pennies [ ] quarters
[ ] nickels [ ] dimes            [ ] nickels [ ] dimes

5.
[ ] pennies [ ] quarters  **$0.55**  [ ] pennies [ ] quarters
[ ] nickels [ ] dimes            [ ] nickels [ ] dimes

**b.** **Brain Stretch:** Use exactly 6 coins to make $0.48.

[ ] pennies  [ ] quarters  [ ] nickels  [ ] dimes

53

# Missing Coins

**a.** Write and draw the missing coins to complete each number sentence.

1.

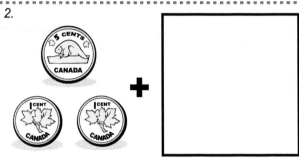

25 ¢ + _____ = 30 ¢

2.

7 ¢ + _____ = 22 ¢

3.

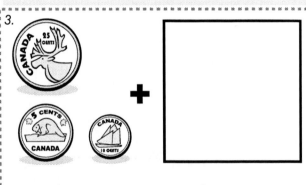

40 ¢ + _____ = 80 ¢

4.

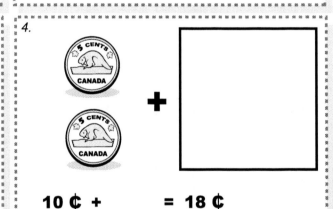

10 ¢ + _____ = 18 ¢

5.

50 ¢ + _____ = $ 1.00

6.

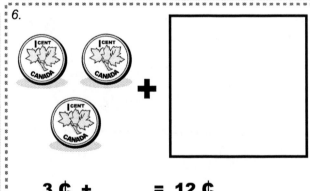

3 ¢ + _____ = 12 ¢

Canadian Math Basics Series  Grade 2

# Shopping At A Pet Store

**a.** Answer the following questions.

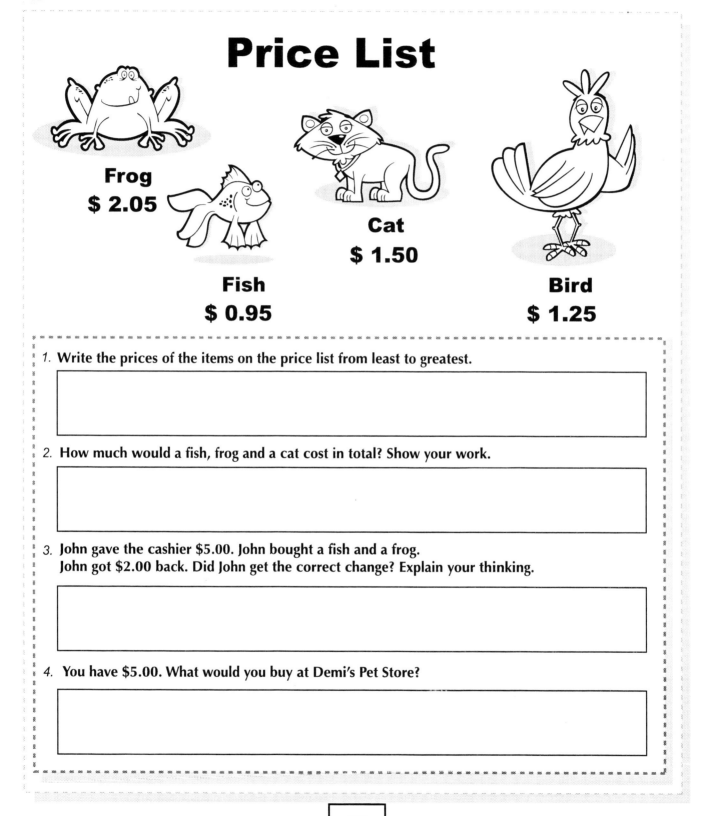

## Price List

**Frog**
**$ 2.05**

**Fish**
**$ 0.95**

**Cat**
**$ 1.50**

**Bird**
**$ 1.25**

*1.* Write the prices of the items on the price list from least to greatest.

*2.* How much would a fish, frog and a cat cost in total? Show your work.

*3.* John gave the cashier $5.00. John bought a fish and a frog.
John got $2.00 back. Did John get the correct change? Explain your thinking.

*4.* You have $5.00. What would you buy at Demi's Pet Store?

Chalkboard Publishing Inc © 2007

Canadian Math Basics Series  Grade 2

# Non Standard Measuring

**a.** How long is each object? Count the feet and record.

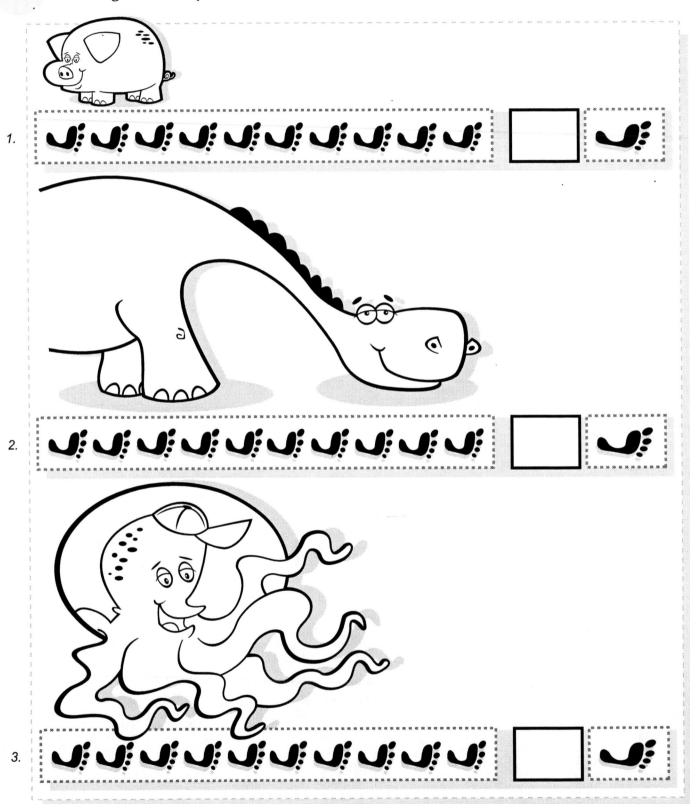

Chalkboard Publishing Inc © 2007

Canadian Math Basics Series Grade 2

# Exploring Centimetres

**a.** Write the length of each object in centimetres.

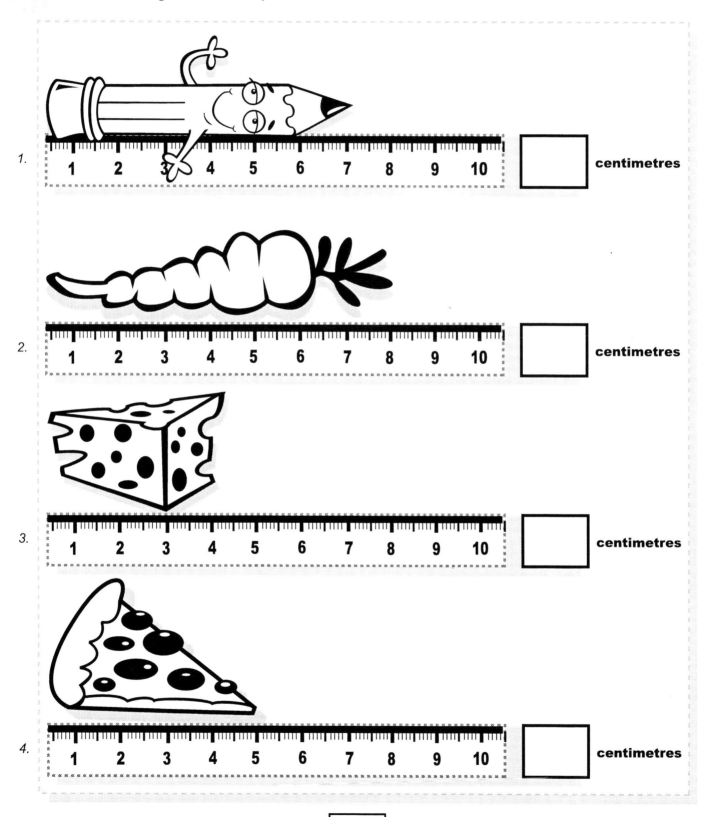

1. ☐ centimetres

2. ☐ centimetres

3. ☐ centimetres

4. ☐ centimetres

Canadian Math Basics Series  Grade 2

# Exploring Centimetres

**a.** Write the length of each object in centimetres.

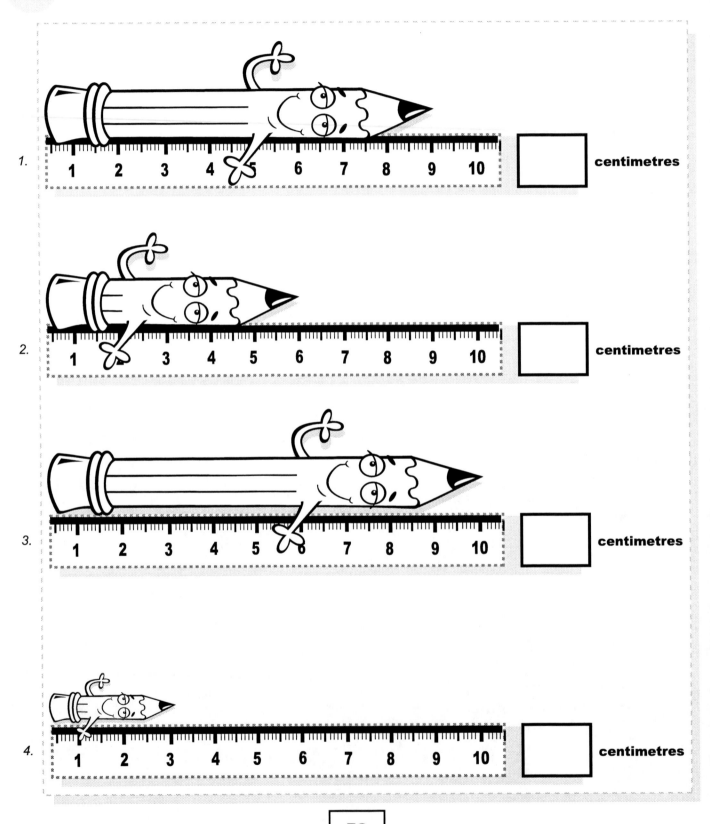

1. centimetres

2. centimetres

3. centimetres

4. centimetres

**Canadian Math Basics Series  Grade 2**

# Exploring Centimetres

**a.** Write the length of each object in centimetres.

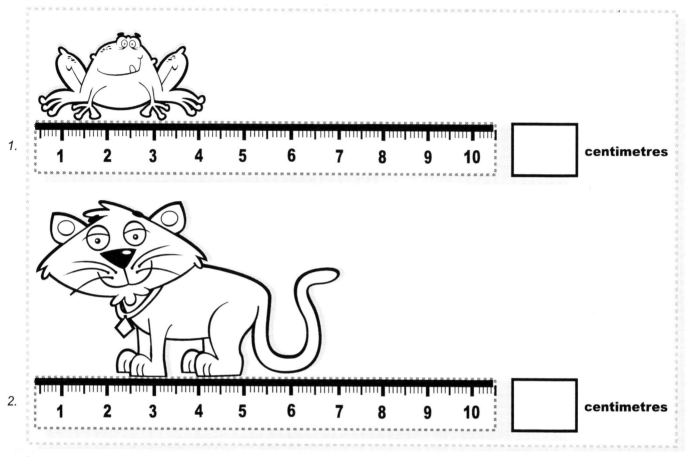

1. [ ] centimetres

2. [ ] centimetres

**b. Brain Stretch:** About how many cubes long is the caterpillar?

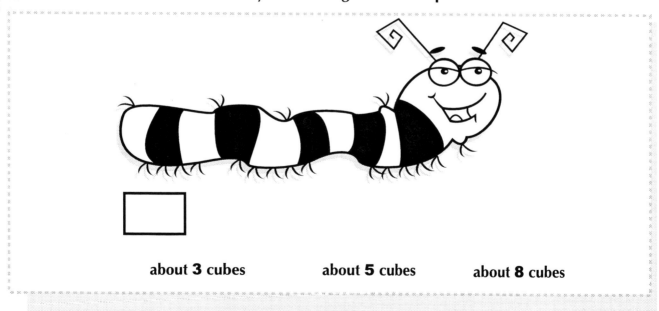

[ ]

about **3** cubes        about **5** cubes        about **8** cubes

**Canadian Math Basics Series  Grade 2**

# Exploring Weight

**a.** How much does each germ weigh?

1. [ ] **blocks**

2. [ ] **blocks**

3. [ ] **blocks**

4. [ ] **blocks**

5. [ ] **blocks**

6. [ ] **blocks**

7. [ ] **blocks**

8. [ ] **blocks**

9. [ ] **blocks**

Canadian Math Basics Series  Grade 2

# Exploring Capacity

**a.** Colour the container that holds more.

1.

2.

3.

4.

5.

6.

7.

8.

9.

10.

Canadian Math Basics Series  Grade 2

# Exploring Measurement

**a.** Match the measurement tool you would use for each activity.

1. You need to measure a cup of sugar for a cake.

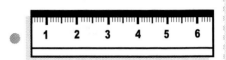

2. You want to know the temperature.

3. You want to measure the length of your book.

4. You want to weigh some apples.

5. You want to know what time it is.

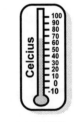

6. You want to know the date.

Canadian Math Basics Series  Grade 2

# Exploring Perimeter

**a. Find the perimeter.**

> **Math Talk:** To find the perimeter add the lengths of each side of the figure.
>
>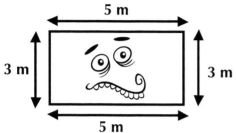
>
> 5 m + 5 m + 3 m + 3 m = 16 m
>
> The perimeter is 16 m.

1.

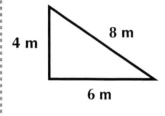

perimeter = ☐

2.

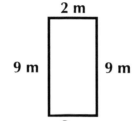

perimeter = ☐

3.

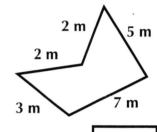

perimeter = ☐

4.

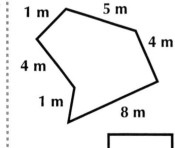

perimeter = ☐

5.

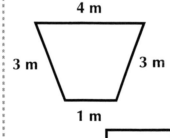

perimeter = ☐

6.

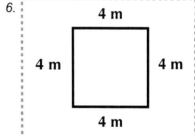

perimeter = ☐

Canadian Math Basics Series  Grade 2

# Exploring Area

**a.** Find the area of each figure.

## Math Talk: Area

Area is the number of units that covers a figure.

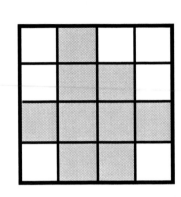

**1 covered square = 1 unit**

**The area = 9 square units**

---

1.

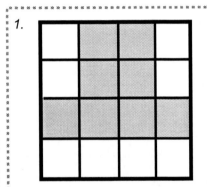

Area = ☐ square units

2.

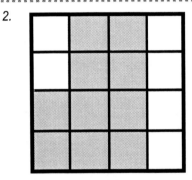

Area = ☐ square units

3.

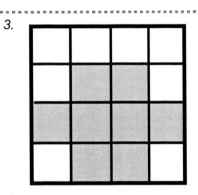

Area = ☐ square units

4.

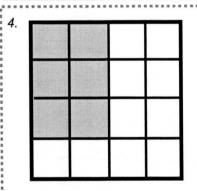

Area = ☐ square units

5.

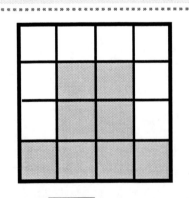

Area = ☐ square units

6.

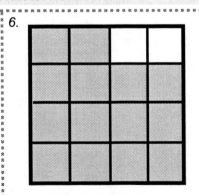

Area = ☐ square units

Canadian Math Basics Series  Grade 2

# Temperature Check

**a.** Is the temperature hot or cold in the picture? Circle your answer.

1.

cold   or   hot

2.

cold   or   hot

3.

cold   or   hot

4.

cold   or   hot

**b.** **Brain Stretch:**

1. What is something you like to do on a **hot** day?

_____

2. What is something you like to do on a **cold** day?

_____

Canadian Math Basics Series  Grade 2

# Reading Pictographs

**a.** Read the pictograph and answer the questions.

### Math Talk: Pictographs

A pictograph shows pictures or icons to represent data and compare information. Pictographs include keys or definitions of the pictures or icons.

Sample:

 = 1 vote

Ms. Richard's class conducted a survey on their favourite way to eat apples. Use the pictograph to answer questions about the results.

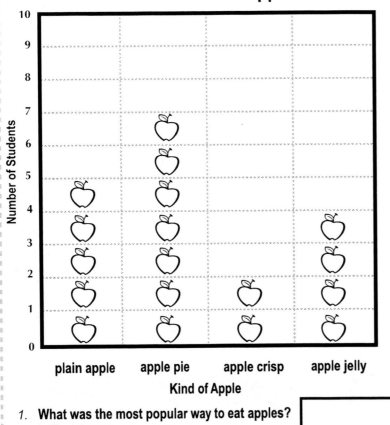

**Favourite Apples**

1. What was the most popular way to eat apples?

2. How many students voted for apple pie?

3. How many students voted altogether?

Chalkboard Publishing Inc © 2007
Canadian Math Basics Series  Grade 2

# Reading Tally Charts

**a.** Answer the questions.

> ## Math Talk: Tally Chart
> A tally chart shows data by counting by groups of five. Each line, or tally represents **1**. Once you reach a group of **5** you start another group.
> 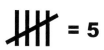 = 5

**A.**

### Favourite Colour

| Colour | Tally | Number |
|--------|-------|--------|
| Green | || | |
| Red | ||||| | |
| Blue | ||||| ||| | |
| Yellow | |||| | |

1. What colour was chosen the most?

2. How many people chose red?

3. How many people chose either green or blue?

**B.**

### Favourite Vegetable

| Vegetable | Tally | Number |
|-----------|-------|--------|
| Carrots | ||||| | |
| Cucumbers | ||||| | |
| Green Beans | ||||| ||| | |
| Lettuce | || | |

1. What vegetable was chosen the most?

2. How many more people chose carrots than lettuce?

3. If 6 more people chose cucumbers, how many people would have chosen cucumbers in total?"

**C.**

### Favourite Cookie

| Cookie | Tally | Number |
|--------|-------|--------|
| Chocolate Chip | || | |
| Peanut Butter | ||||| | |
| Double Chocolate | ||||| | |

1. How many people chose double chocolate as their favourite cookie?

2. How many more people chose peanut butter than chocolate chip?

Chalkboard Publishing Inc © 2007

Canadian Math Basics Series  Grade 2

# Exploring Bar Graphs

**a.** Ms. Demitt conducted a class survey on favourite recess activities. Read the graph and answer the questions.

**Math Talk: Bar Graphs**
Horizontal or vertical bars in a graph that display data.

## Favourite Recess Activity

Activity:
- Skipping
- Basketball
- Baseball
- Hopscotch
- Tag

Number of Students    1   2   3   4   5   6   7   8   9   10

1. The most popular recess activity is: _____

2. The least popular recess activity is: _____

3. _____ students liked hopscotch.

4. _____ more students liked tag over basketball.

5. What is your favourite recess activity?

_____

Chalkboard Publishing Inc © 2007                    Canadian Math Basics Series  Grade 2

# Exploring Bar Graphs

**a.** Mr. Wong's class did a survey on students' favourite germs. Use the data from the bar graph to answer the questions.

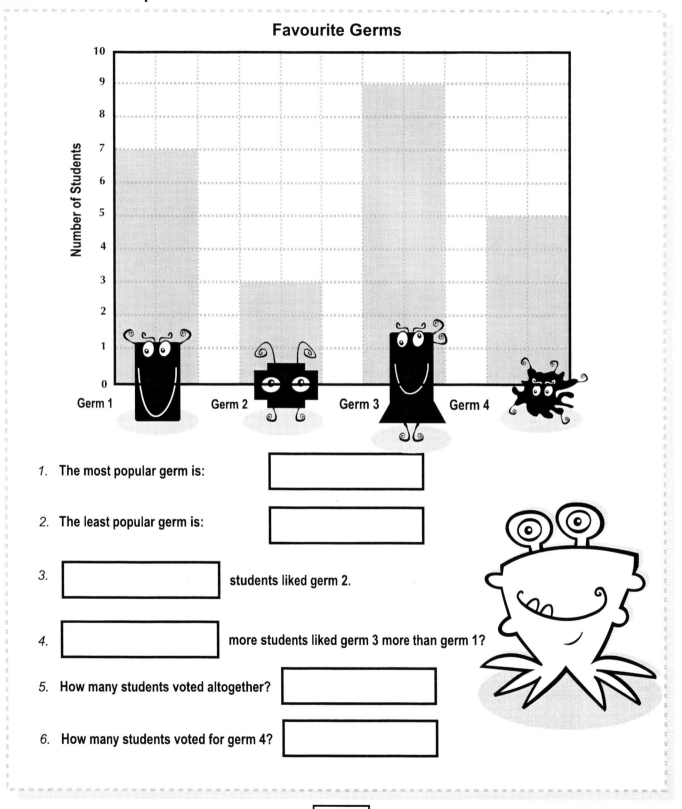

Favourite Germs

1. The most popular germ is:

2. The least popular germ is:

3. _____ students liked germ 2.

4. _____ more students liked germ 3 more than germ 1?

5. How many students voted altogether?

6. How many students voted for germ 4?

Chalkboard Publishing Inc © 2007

Canadian Math Basics Series Grade 2

# Exploring Bar Graphs

**a.** Use data from the frequency table to make a bar graph. Answer the questions.

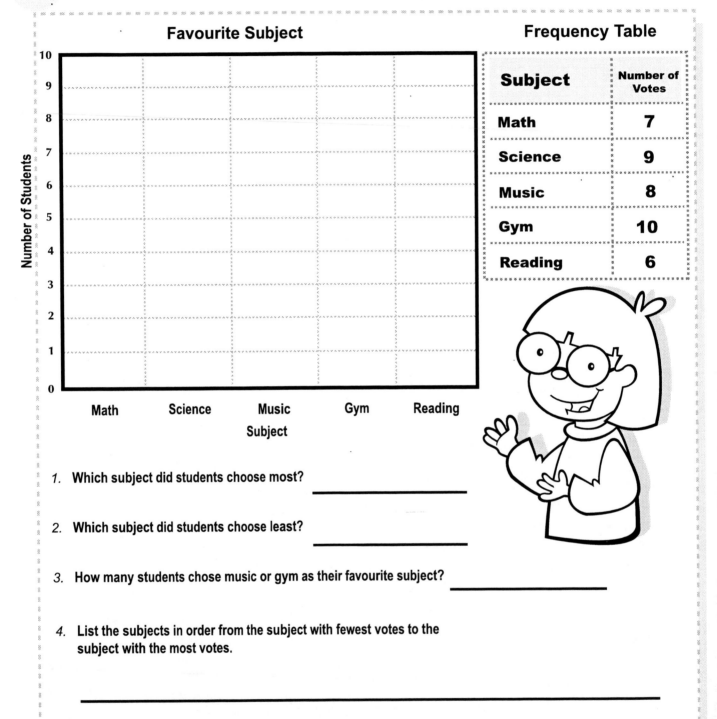

**Favourite Subject**

**Frequency Table**

| Subject | Number of Votes |
|---------|-----------------|
| Math | 7 |
| Science | 9 |
| Music | 8 |
| Gym | 10 |
| Reading | 6 |

1. Which subject did students choose most? _____

2. Which subject did students choose least? _____

3. How many students chose music or gym as their favourite subject? _____

4. List the subjects in order from the subject with fewest votes to the subject with the most votes.

_____

5. How many students chose either math or science? _____

Canadian Math Basics Series  Grade 2

# Exploring Probability

**a. Answer the questions.**

1. What germ would be **most** likely picked without looking?  Circle your answer.

2. What germ would be **least** likely picked without looking?  Circle your answer.

3. What germ would be **most** likely picked without looking? Circle your answer.  Circle your answer.

4. What germ would be **least** likely picked without looking?  Circle your answer.

5. What germ would be **most** likely picked without looking?  Circle your answer.

6. What germ would be **least** likely picked without looking?  Circle your answer.

Canadian Math Basics Series  Grade 2

# Exploring Polygons

a. Learn about polygons.

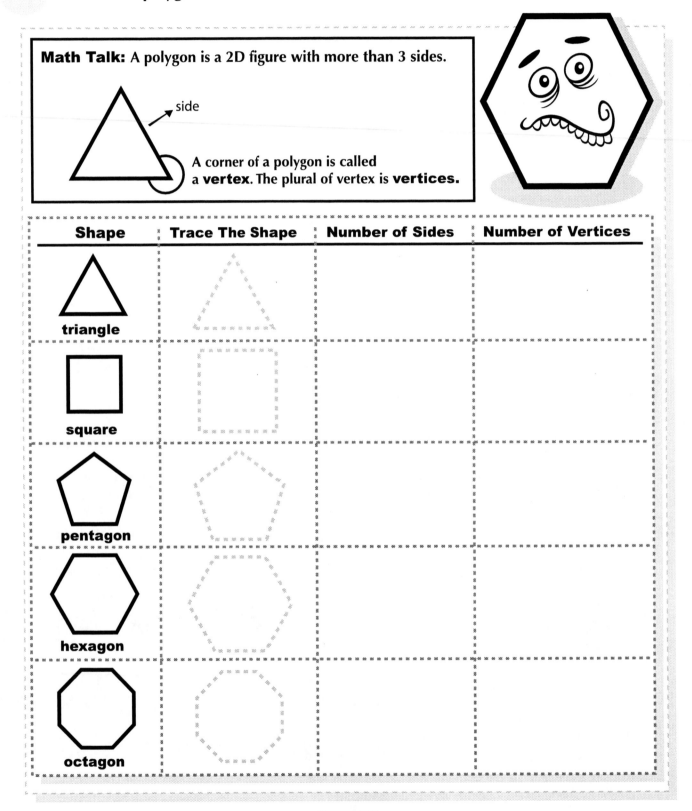

**Math Talk:** A polygon is a 2D figure with more than 3 sides.

side

A corner of a polygon is called a **vertex**. The plural of vertex is **vertices**.

| Shape | Trace The Shape | Number of Sides | Number of Vertices |
|---|---|---|---|
| triangle | | | |
| square | | | |
| pentagon | | | |
| hexagon | | | |
| octagon | | | |

Canadian Math Basics Series  Grade 2

# Identifying 2D Figures

**a.** Look at the picture. Use the colour key to colour the picture.

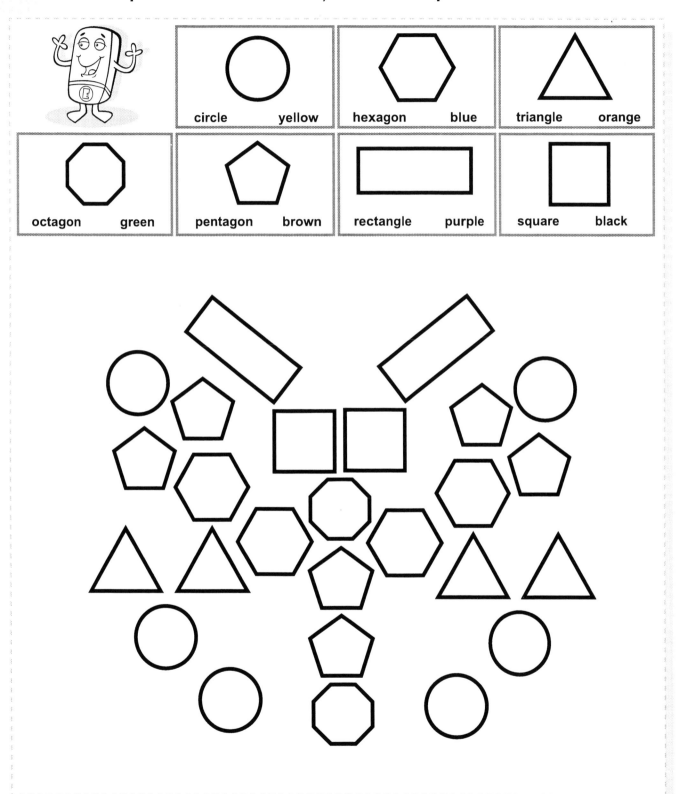

| circle | yellow | hexagon | blue | triangle | orange |

| octagon | green | pentagon | brown | rectangle | purple | square | black |

Chalkboard Publishing Inc © 2007  Canadian Math Basics Series  Grade 2

# Sorting 2D Figures

**a. Read the rule. Colour the shapes that follow that rule.**

Shapes with **more** than **4 vertices.**

1.

Shapes with **4 sides.**

2.

Shapes with **less** than **5 sides.**

3.

Shapes with **more** than **3 sides.**

4.

Shapes with **less** then **5 vertices.**

5.

Chalkboard Publishing Inc © 2007

Canadian Math Basics Series  Grade 2

# Identifying 3D Figures

**a.** Match the name of each 3D figure.

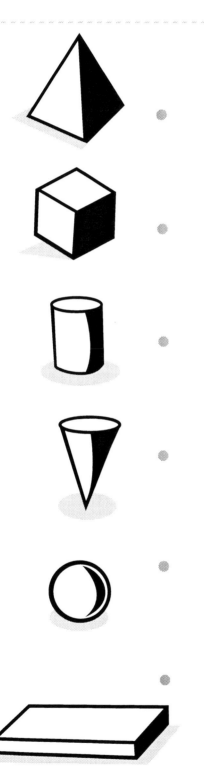

- pyramid
- cylinder
- sphere
- rectangular prism
- cone
- cube

# Identifying 3D Figures

**a.** Match the name of each 3D figure to an object(s) that looks like it.

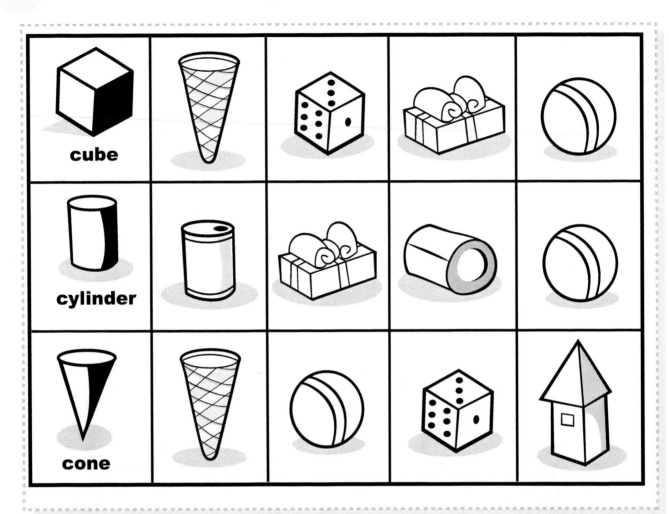

**b.** **Brain Stretch:** Circle the 3D figure that you can make from the pieces.

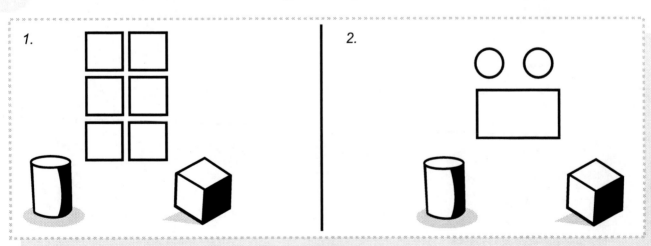

Canadian Math Basics Series  Grade 2

# Sorting 3D Figures

**a.** Use each rule to sort the 3 dimensional figures.

Circle the 3D figures that can be **stacked** on each other.

1.

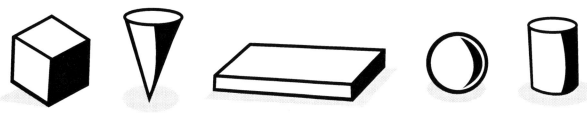

Circle the 3D figures that **cannot** be stacked on each other.

2.

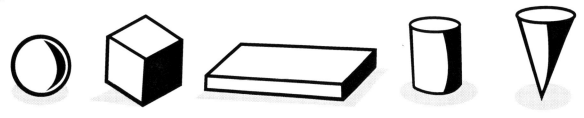

Circle the 3D figures that can **roll.**

3.

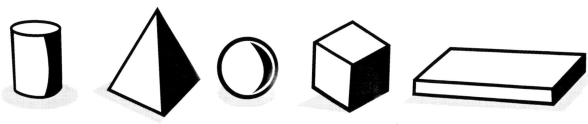

Circle the 3D figures that **cannot roll.**

4.

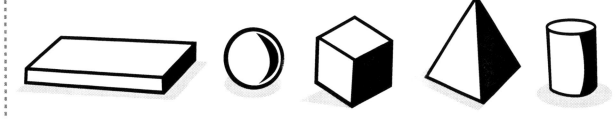

Chalkboard Publishing Inc © 2007

# Exploring Symmetry

**a.** Do these two parts match and have the same size and shape?

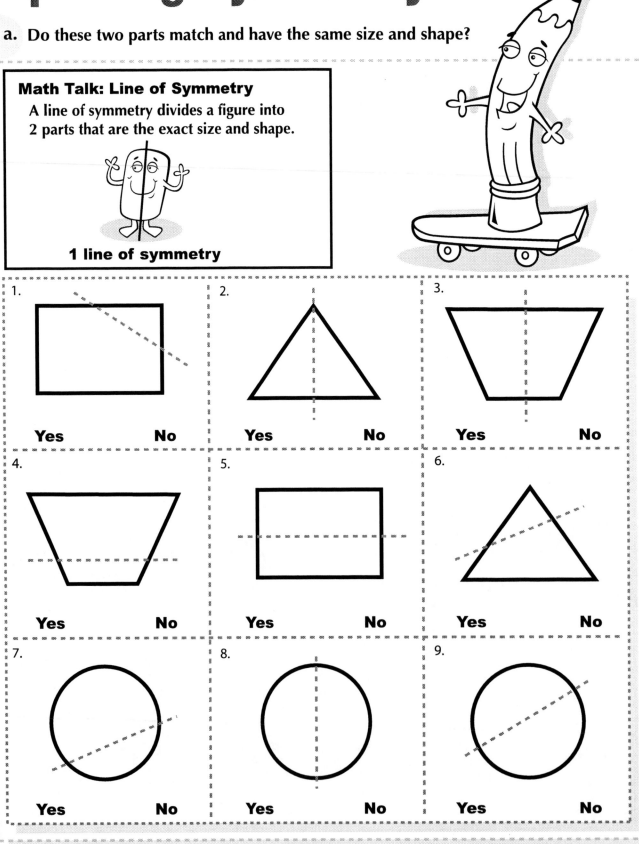

**Math Talk: Line of Symmetry**

A line of symmetry divides a figure into 2 parts that are the exact size and shape.

**1 line of symmetry**

1.

Yes        No

2.

Yes        No

3.

Yes        No

4.

Yes        No

5.

Yes        No

6.

Yes        No

7.

Yes        No

8.

Yes        No

9.

Yes        No

Canadian Math Basics Series  Grade 2

# Exploring Symmetry

**a.** Draw the other half of this picture.

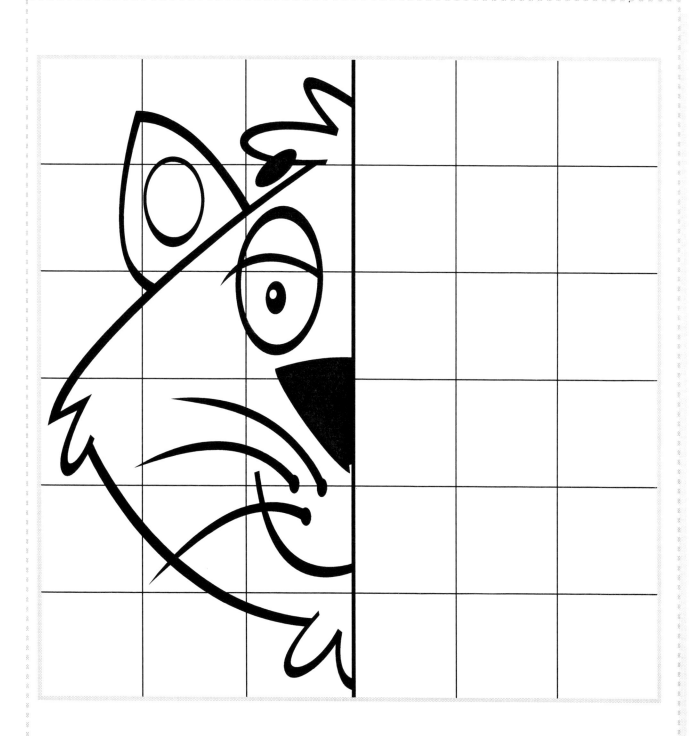

Canadian Math Basics Series  Grade 2

# Following Directions

**a.** Read and colour the picture.

Colour the bird on **top** of the dinosaur blue.
Colour the sun to the **left** of the trees yellow.
Colour the caterpillar **under** the dinosaur red.
Colour the dinosaur **next to** the caterpillar purple.
Colour the grass **under** the caterpillar green.

Canadian Math Basics Series  Grade 2

# Following Directions

**a.** Read and colour the picture.

Colour the stars on **top** of the moon yellow.
Colour the moon to the **left** of the spaceship blue.
Colour the planet **under** the robot orange.
Colour the robot **next to** the spaceship green.

Chalkboard Publishing Inc © 2007
Canadian Math Basics Series  Grade 2

# Exploring Coordinates

**a.** Look at the grid of germs and name the following coordinates.

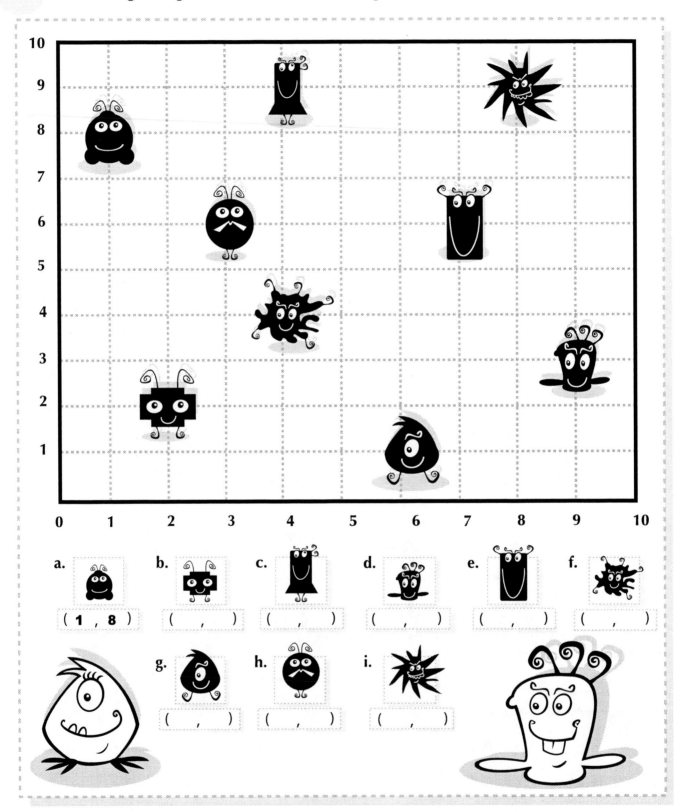

a.  ( **1** , **8** )

b.  ( , )

c.  ( , )

d.  ( , )

e.  ( , )

f.  ( , )

g.  ( , )

h.  ( , )

i.  ( , )

Canadian Math Basics Series  Grade 2

# Exploring Patterns

**a.** Finish the patterns on the grid.

1.
2.
3.
4.
5.

**Chalkboard Publishing Inc © 2007**

**Canadian Math Basics Series  Grade 2**

# Exploring Patterns

**a.** Draw the shape that comes next in each pattern.

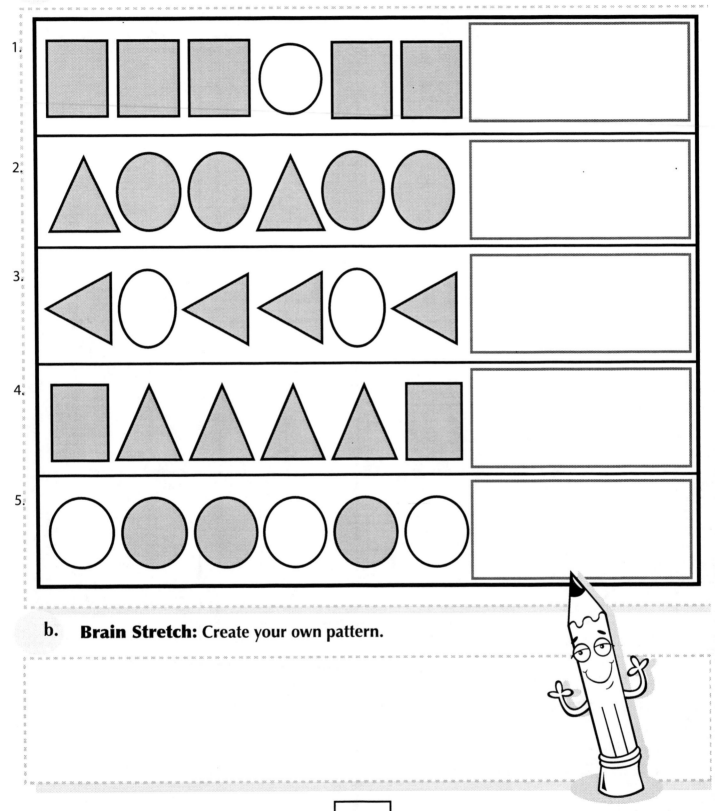

**b.** **Brain Stretch:** Create your own pattern.

Canadian Math Basics Series  Grade 2

# Input Charts

a. Complete the charts by filling in the missing numbers.

1.

| + 4 | |
|---|---|
| Input | Output |
| 1 | |
| 2 | |
| | 7 |
| 4 | |

2.

| + 2 | |
|---|---|
| Input | Output |
| 2 | |
| | 8 |
| 3 | |
| 7 | |

3.

| - 1 | |
|---|---|
| Input | Output |
| 7 | |
| 2 | |
| | 4 |
| | 3 |

4.

| - 3 | |
|---|---|
| Input | Output |
| 10 | |
| | 2 |
| 7 | |
| 9 | |

5.

| + 5 | |
|---|---|
| Input | Output |
| 3 | |
| 2 | |
| | 10 |
| | 6 |

6.

| + 10 | |
|---|---|
| Input | Output |
| 4 | |
| | 12 |
| 5 | |
| 10 | |

Canadian Math Basics Series  Grade 2

# Number Patterns

**a.** Complete the charts by filling in the missing numbers.

1. 100, 90, 80, 70, 60, 50, 40, ☐ , ☐ , ☐

   Pattern Rule _____

2. 5, 10, 15, 20, 25, ☐ , ☐ , ☐

   Pattern Rule _____

3. 2, 4, 6, 8, 10, ☐ , ☐ , ☐

   Pattern Rule _____

4. 10, 20, 30, 40, 50, ☐ , ☐ , ☐

   Pattern Rule _____

5. 3, 6, 9, 12, ☐ , ☐ , ☐

   Pattern Rule _____

Canadian Math Basics Series  Grade 2

# More Word Problems

**a.** Complete the following word problems.

| Word Problems | Show Your Work |
|---|---|
| **1.** Carrie saw **14** ladybugs. Larry saw **25** ladybugs. How many ladybugs did they see in all? <br><br> They saw _____ ladybugs. | |
| **2.** There are **86** frogs in the pond. **19** frogs hopped away. How many frogs are left in the pond? <br><br> _____ frogs are left. | |
| **3.** There were **31** cookies in the jar. Mike ate **24** of them. How many cookies were left? <br><br> There were _____ cookies left. | |
| **4.** Chris had **27** video games. He bought 14 more. How many video games does he have altogether? <br><br> He has _____ video games all together. | |

Canadian Math Basics Series  Grade 2

# Certificate Of Completion

# Great Work!

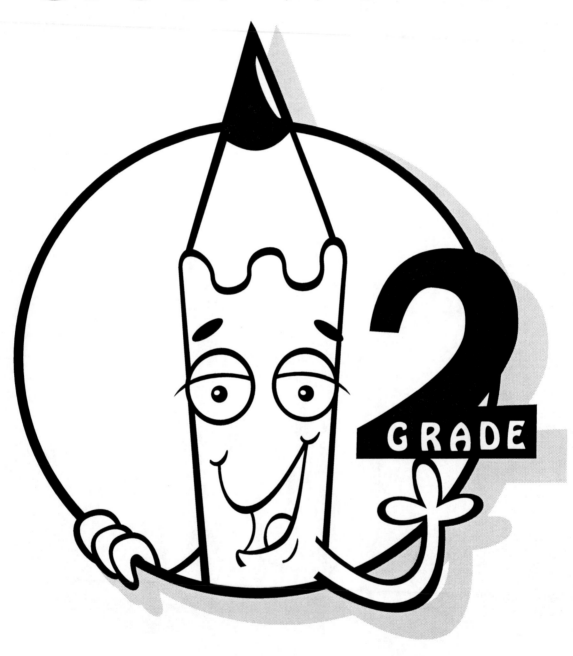

GRADE 2

Canadian Math Basics Series  Grade 2

# Answer Pages

pg. 2

```
o a s e v e n t e e n n
n e i g h t e e n b c i
e e n i n e t e e n v n
s i a e l e v e n z a e
e g z t w e l v e z f m
v h g o t o t h e z o o
e t q f i f t e e n q i
n q q t w e n t y a b a
a f o u r t e e n t w o
s i x t e e n t h r e e
s i x t h i r t e e n w
f o u r a f i v e t e n
```

pg.3.   b.   60, 70, 80, 90, 100, 110, 120, 130, 140
15, 20, 25, 30, 35, 40, 45, 50, 55
150, 152, 154, 156, 158, 160, 162, 164, 166

p.4.   b.   57, 58, 59, 60, 61, 62

67, 68, 69,

p.5. orange = 2, 8, 10, 20, 32, 44, 70, 78, 84, 90, 100, 136, 176
green = 7, 13, 27, 37, 51, 71, 75, 77, 83, 85, 89, 91, 133, 167

p.6.   a.   1. 81     2. 64     3. 13     4. 88, 90

5. 5     6. 18     7. 70     8. 39, 41

9. 35     10. 55

b.   1. 18, 29, 54, 71
2. 3, 39, 63, 84
3. 6, 46, 69, 92

c.   1. 71, 46, 24
2. 19, 15, 11

p.7.   a.   1.   2 tens, 8 ones  28
2.   4 tens, 5 ones  45
3.   1 ten, 9 ones  19
4.   2 tens, 6 ones  26
5.   1 ten, 7 ones  17
6.   3 tens, 0 ones  30
7.   2 tens, 3 ones  23
8.   2 tens, 0 ones  20
9.   4 tens, 0 ones  40

p.8.   a.   1.   4 tens, 4 ones, 44
2.   8 tens, 0 ones, 80
3.   3 tens, 1 ones, 31
4.   2 tens, 2 ones, 22
5.   6 tens, 2 ones, 62
6.   1 tens, 5 ones, 15
7.   0 tens, 4 ones, 4
8.   4 tens, 9 ones, 49
9.   8 tens, 5 ones, 85

b.   1. 49   2. 89   3. 28   4. 25

Chalkboard Publishing Inc © 2007   Canadian Math Basics Series  Grade 2

# Answer Pages

p.9.    a.    1.    40 +1, blocks
             2.    blocks, 2 tens and 9 ones
             3.    1 ten and 6 ones, 10+6
             4.    blocks, 5 tens and 3 ones
             5.    blocks, 90 + 0

p. 10.  a.    1. 45      2. 76      3. 19      4. 62
             5. 84      6. 11      7. 56      8. 8
             9. 53      10. 4      11. 39     12. 84

p. 11.  a.    1. 9       2. 12      3. 9       4. 8
             5. 1       6. 14      7. 6       8. 4
             9. 14      10. 10     11. 5      12. 3
             13. 7      14. 8      15. 11     16. 20
             17. 10     18. 18

p.12.   a.    1. 3       2. 9       3. 9       4. 5
             5. 6       6. 6       7. 8       8. 9
             9. 10      10. 0      11. 10     12. 5
             13. 2      14. 4      15. 5      16. 8
             17. 10     18. 6

p. 13.  a     B = 20     T = 7      E = 6      D = 10
             W = 14     C = 9      G = 4      L = 15
             A = 12     Y = 3      U = 8      N = 13
             S = 16     I = 18     H = 11     R = 17

        Because her students were really bright!

        b.    1. 17      2. 14      3. 13      4. 12

p. 14.  a.    1. 6       2. 3       3. 9       4. 3
             5. 8       6. 8       7. 3       8. 7
             9. 6       10. 1      11. 8      12. 6
             13. 6      14. 1      15. 9      16. 10
             17. 8      18. 3

p. 15.  a.    1. 9       2. 4       3. 10      4. 4
             5. 5       6. 8       7. 8       8. 6
             9. 7       10. 8      11. 9      12. 7
             13. 10     14. 7      15. 1      16. 6
             17. 6      18. 7

b. Answers may vary. 1.  2 + 6 = 8   6 + 2 = 8   8 - 2 = 6   8 - 6 = 2
                     2.  3 + 7 = 10   7 + 3 = 10   10 - 3 = 7   10 - 7 = 3

Canadian Math Basics Series  Grade 2

# Answer Pages

| p. 16. | a. | 1. 7 | 2. 4 | 3. 1 | 4. 8 |
| | | 5. 7 | 6. 7 | 7. 6 | 8. 4 |
| | | 9. 10 | 10. 10 | 11. 5 | 12. 3 |
| | | 13. 3 | 14. 8 | 15. 1 | 16. 1 |
| | | 17. 9 | 18. 1 | | |
| | | | | | |
| | b. | 1. 5 | 2. 4 | 3. 4 | 4. 9 |
| | | | | | |
| p. 17. | a. | 1. 4 | 2. 2 | 3. 9 | 4. 3 |
| | | 5. 15 | 6. 3 | 7. 3 | 8. 7 |
| | | 9. 0 | 10. 8 | 11. 30 | 12. 15 |
| | | 13. 9 | 14. 6 | 15. 5 | 16. 17 |
| | | 17. 1 | 18. 14 | | |

p. 18.  a.  R=8   B=3   I=2   O=4   N=5   W=1   A=6   A rainbow!

   b.  sixteen= 16   four= 4   twelve=12   nine= 9   eighteen=18

p. 19.  a.
1.   $11 - 5 = 6$
2.   $12 - 8 = 4$
3.   $6 + 9 = 15$
4.   $18 - 8 = 10$
5.   $12 - 5 = 7$
6.   $3 + 7 = 10$
7.   $14 - 5 = 9$

| | b. | 1. 5 | 2. 15 | 3. 6 | 4. 14 | 5. 11 |
| | | | | | | |
| p. 20. | a. | 1. 29 | 2. 19 | 3. 11 | 4. 22 | 5. 27 |
| | | 6. 20 | 7. 13 | 8. 21 | 9. 28 | 10. 21 |
| | | 11. 25 | 12. 18 | 13. 25 | 14. 22 | 15. 7 |
| | | 16. 19 | | | | |
| | | | | | | |
| p. 21. | a. | 1. 85 | 2. 37 | 3. 98 | 4. 97 | 5. 74 |
| | | 6. 62 | 7. 88 | 8. 85 | 9. 95 | 10. 46 |
| | | 11. 87 | 12. 57 | 13. 64 | 14. 99 | 15. 44 |
| | | 16. 97 | 17. 52 | 18. 48 | 19. 33 | 20. 95 |

p.22.  a.  I=97   R=42   W=78   L=92   H= 25
   T= 85   V= 73   U= 65   G= 32   X= 71
   E= 84   O= 74   A= 66   B= 96   S= 59
   N= 53   He was learning a new language

| p.23. | a. | 1. 82 | 2. 41 | 3. 102 | 4. 61 | 5. 82 |
| | | 6. 70 | 7. 90 | 8. 81 | 9. 62 | 10. 72 |
| | | 11. 71 | 12. 61 | 13. 50 | 14. 100 | 15. 44 |
| | | | | | | |
| p. 24. | a. | 1. 71 | 2. 84 | 3. 94 | 4. 40 | 5. 74 |
| | | 6. 73 | 7. 90 | 8. 82 | 9. 65 | 10. 81 |
| | | 11. 82 | 12. 82 | 13. 72 | 14. 91 | 15. 96 |

   b.  1. 20, $5 + 5 + 5 + 5 = 20$
      2. 9, $3 + 3 + 3 = 9$

**Canadian Math Basics Series  Grade 2**

# Answer Pages

| p.25. | a. | 1. 45 | 2. 44 | 3. 16 | 4. 44 | 5. 24 |
|---|---|---|---|---|---|---|
| | | 6. 55 | 7. 64 | 8. 12 | 9. 44 | 10. 71 |
| | | 11. 22 | 12. 26 | 13. 10 | 14. 11 | 15. 20 |
| | | 16. 55 | 17. 2 | 18. 75 | 19. 51 | 20. 2 |

| p.26. | a. | 1. 14 | 2. 44 | 3. 67 | 4. 16 | 5. 51 |
|---|---|---|---|---|---|---|
| | | 6. 3 | 7. 31 | 8. 22 | 9. 34 | 10. 11 |
| | | 11. 28 | | | | |

| p.27. | a. | 1. 36 | 2. 57 | 3. 37 | 4. 9 | 5. 7 |
|---|---|---|---|---|---|---|
| | | 6. 17 | 7. 27 | 8. 17 | 9. 36 | 10. 19 |
| | | 11. 8 | 12. 57 | 13. 17 | 14. 58 | 15. 11 |
| | | 16. 13 | 17. 19 | 18. 7 | 19. 36 | 20. 18 |

| p.28. | a. | E=7 | P=12 | H=29 | N=38 | U=58 | W=16 | O=13 | T=47 | S=69 |
|---|---|---|---|---|---|---|---|---|---|---|
| | | Z=5 | M=44 | I=25 | | | | | | |

When someone steps on its mouse!

| p.29. | a. | 1. 62 | 2. 18 | 3. 46 | 4. 66 | |
|---|---|---|---|---|---|---|

| p.30. | a. | 1. 12 | 2. 6 | 3. 20 | 4. 12 | 5. 14 |
|---|---|---|---|---|---|---|
| | | 6. 16 | | | | |

| p. 31. | a. | 1. 5+5+5=15 | 3x5=15 |
|---|---|---|---|
| | | 2. 8+8=16 | 2x8=16 |
| | | 3. 7+7=14 | 2x7=14 |
| | | 4. 3+3+3+3+3=15 | 5x3=15 |
| | | 5. 9+9=18 | 2x9=18 |
| | | 6. 4+4+4+4=16 | 4x4=16 |
| | | 7. 5+5+5+5=20 | 4x5=20 |
| | | 8. 10+10=20 | 2x10=20 |
| | | 9. 2+2+2+2+2=10 | 5x2=10 |

| p.32. | a. | 1. 9, 18 | 2. 8, 40 | 3. 5, 50 |
|---|---|---|---|---|

p.33.　a.
1. one and three
2. one
3. two and three
4. two
5. one and three
6. three
7. one and two

| p.34. | a. | 1. 1/2 | 2. 1/3 | 3. 1/3 | 4. 1/2 | 5. 1/2 |
|---|---|---|---|---|---|---|
| | | 6. 1/4 | 7. 1/3 | 8. 1/4 | 9. 1/3 | 10. 1/3 |
| | | 11. 1/4 | 12. 1/4 | | | |

| p.35. | a. | 1. 6/7 | 2. 1/8 | 3. 1/2 | 4. 3/4 | 5. 5/9 |
|---|---|---|---|---|---|---|
| | | 6. 8/9 | 7. 1/5 | 8. 3/5 | 9. 1/2 | 10. 2/3 |
| | | 11. 2/8 | 12. 2/6 | 13. 4/7 | 14. 1/3 | 15. 4/6 |
| | | 16. 1/4 | 17. 1/2 | 18. 7/8 | | |

　　　　　　　　　　Canadian Math Basics Series  Grade 2

# Answer Pages

p.36.       answers may vary

1.     2.     3.     4.     5.     6.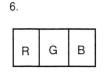

p.37.    a.      colour one germ in each question

p.38.    a.      1. Alex could share with three friends.      2. 2/3 of Megan's sweaters are old.    3. She gave away two pieces.
                  4. She gave away 3/4 of her bubble gum.      5. Each person will get one cookie.

p.39.    a.

| | | | |
|---|---|---|---|
| 1. 6, 6:00 | 2. 11, 11:00 | 3. 5, 5:00 | 4. 2, 2:00 |
| 5. 10, 10:00 | 6. 8, 8:00 | 7. 4, 4:00 | 8. 9, 9:00 |
| 9. 12, 12:00 | 10. 7, 7:00 | 11. 1, 1:00 | 12. 3, 3:00 |

p. 40.    a.

| | | | |
|---|---|---|---|
| 1. 8, 8:30 | 2. 1, 1:30 | 3. 6, 6:30 | 4. 2, 2:30 |
| 5. 11, 11:30 | 6. 3, 3:30 | 7. 7, 7:30 | 8. 12, 12:30 |
| 9. 4, 4:30 | 10. 9, 9:30 | 11. 10, 10:30 | 12. 5, 5:30 |

p. 41.    a.

| | | | |
|---|---|---|---|
| 1. 12, 12:15 | 2. 1, 1:15 | 3. 2, 2:15 | 4. 5, 5:15 |
| 5. 6, 6:15 | 6. 7, 7:15 | 7. 9, 9:15 | 8. 4, 4:15 |
| 9. 10, 10:15 | 10. 9, 9:15 | 11. 11, 11:15 | 12. 4, 4:15 |

p.42.    a.

| | | | |
|---|---|---|---|
| 1. 1, 12:45 | 2. 2, 1:45 | 3. 3, 2:45 | 4. 6, 5:45 |
| 5. 7, 6:45 | 6. 8, 7:45 | 7. 10, 9:45 | 8. 5, 4:45 |
| 9. 11, 10:45 | 10. 1, 12:45 | 11. 12, 11:45 | 12. 4, 3:45 |

p.43.    a.      4:00    7:30      8:00      11:00     3:00     3:30      10:30     5:00
                 12:30    9:30      4:30      2:00

p.44.

2:15      8:00      10:30      9:30      3:15      6:00

4:45      11:30      12:45      7:45      9:00      1:30

p.45.    a.

| | | | | |
|---|---|---|---|---|
| January | February | March | April | May |
| June | July | August | September | October |
| November | December | | | |

     12, August, answers may vary

p.46.    a.      1. Thursday      2. 5 Tuesdays      3. 4 Saturdays      4. April 7
                  5. April 18       6. Saturday

                  1. 31 days       2. Friday       3. Thursday      4. 4 Fridays

**Canadian Math Basics Series Grade 2**

# Answer Pages

p.47.  a.  9:00    10:00    1hr
            10:30    12:30    2 hrs

            1. hours            2. minutes

p.48.  a.  penny, 1¢
            nickel,  5 ¢
            dime,    10 ¢
            quarter, 25 ¢
            loonie, $1.00
            toonie, $2.00

p.49.  a.  fish= loonie
            cat= 3rd picture of coins
            spaceship= 4th picture of coins
            dinosaur= 2nd picture of coins
            frog=  1st picture of coins

p.50.  a.  sandwich= 5th picture
            pizza= 4th picture
            donut= 3rd picture
            milk= 2nd picture
            fries= 1st picture

p.51.  a.  2. $0.25, $0.25, $0.25, $0.10, $0.05 = $0.90
            3. $0.10, $0.05, $0.05, $0.01, $0.01= $0.22
            4. $0.25, $0.05, $0.05, $0.01, $0.10= $0.46
            5. Rob
            6. Carolyn

p.52.  a.  1. $0.25, $0.10, $0.10, $0.10, $0.10= $0.65
            2. $0.25, $0.05, $0.10, $0.10, $0.01= $0.51
            3. $0.25, $0.25, $0.25, $0.05, $0.01= $0.81
            4. $0.25, $0.10, $0.05. $0.05. $0.01= $0.46
            5. Rafat
            6. George

p.53.      answers may vary

       a.  1.    3 dimes, 2 pennies              1 quarter, 1 nickel, 2 pennies
            2.    2 quarters, 1 nickel, 1 penny    5 dimes, 1 nickel, 1 penny
            3.    3 quarters, 1 dimes, 4 pennies   3 quarters, 2 nickels, 4 pennies
            4.    1 quarter, 2 dimes, 3 pennies    4 dimes, 1 nickel, 3 pennies
            5.    2 quarters, 1 nickel             5 dimes, 5 pennies

       b.  1 quarter, 2 dimes, 3 pennies

p.54.      Drawings of coins may vary.

       a.    1. 5¢        2. 15¢        3. 40¢        4. 8¢        5. 50¢
            6. 9¢

Canadian Math Basics Series  Grade 2

# Answer Pages

p.55.   a.    1. $0.95, $1.25, $1.50, $2.05
                   2. $4.50
                   3. yes
                   4. Answers may vary.

p.56.   a.    1. 3 feet        2. 10 feet       3. 8 feet

p.57.   a.    1. pencil: 7 cm  2. carrot: 8 cm  3. cheese: 4 cm  4. Pizza: 5 cm

p.58.   a.    1. pencil: 9cm   2. pencil 6 cm  3. pencil 10cm  4. pencil 3 cm

p.59.   a.    1. frog 4 cm    2. cat 7cm
        b.    about 8 cubes

p.60.   a.    1. 10        2. 4        3. 5       4. 6       5. 8
                 6. 7        7. 13      8. 11     9. 12

p.61.   a.    1. pail        2. bowl      3. milk jug    4. pail
                 5. tissue box  6. bottle    7. bowl       8. milk jug
                 9. toys        10. toys

p.62.   a.    1. measuring cup
                 2. thermometer
                 3. ruler
                 4. scale
                 5. clock
                 6. calendar

p.63.   a.    1. 18 m      2. 22 m     3. 19 m
                 4. 23 m      5. 11 m     6. 16 m

p.64.   a.    1. 8         2. 10       3. 8       4. 6       5. 8
                 6. 14

p.65.   a.    1. hot        2. cold      3. hot      4. cold
        b.    answers may vary.

p.66.   a.    1. apple pie    2. 7 students   3. 18 students

p.67.   a.    A. 1. blue     2. 5    3. 10
                 B. 1. green beans     2. 2        3. 11
                 C. 1. 5        2. 2

p.68.   a.    1. skipping    2. baseball    3. 5   4. 5   5. answers may vary

p.69.   a.    1. germ 3      2. germ 2     3. 3 students   4. 2 students   5. 24 students
                 6. 5 students

p.70.   a.    1. gym        2. reading    3. 18
                 4. reading, math, music, science, gym
                 5. 16

Chalkboard Publishing Inc © 2007                           **Canadian Math Basics Series  Grade 2**

# Answer Pages

p.71.  a.  1.  2.  3.  4.  5.  6.

p.72.  a.  triangle= 3,3
square= 4,4
pentagon= 5,5
hexagon= 6,6
octagon= 8,8

p.73.  a.  answers may vary

p.74.  a.  1. pentagon, hexagon
2. square, rectangle, trapezoid
3. square, triangle, trapezoid
4. pentagon, rectangle, octagon
5. rectangle, circle, triangle, rhombus

p.75.  a.  pyramid,  cube, cylinder,  cone,, sphere,  rectangular prism

p.76.  a.  dice
can, roll of paper
ice cream cone

       b.  1. cube          2. cylinder

p.77.  a.  1. rectangular prism, cube, cylinder
2. sphere, cone
3. cylinder, sphere
4. rectangular prism, cube, pyramid

p.78.  a.  1. no   2. yes   3. yes   4. no   5. yes   6. no   7. no   8. yes   9. yes

p.82.  a.  b. 2,2          c. 4,9          d. 9,3          e. 7,6
f. 4,4          g. 6,1          h. 3,6          i. 8,9

p.84.  a.  1. rectangle     2. triangle     3. triangle     4. triangle
5. coloured circle
       b.  answers may vary

p.85.  a.  1. 5, 6, 3, 8
2. 4, 6, 5, 9
3. 6, 1, 5, 4
4. 7, 5, 4, 6
5. 8, 7, 5, 1
6. 14, 2, 15, 20

p.86.  a.  1. 30, 20, 10,     pattern rule:  -10 each time
2. 30, 35, 40,     pattern rule:  +5 each time
3. 12, 14, 16,     pattern rule:  +2 each time
4. 60, 70, 80,     pattern rule:  +10 each time
5. 15, 18, 21,     pattern rule:  +3 each time

p.87.  a. 1. They saw 39 ladybugs.   2. 67 frogs are left.   3. 7 cookies were left.   4. He has 41 video games in all.

**Canadian Math Basics Series  Grade 2**